HOW FOOD TRAVELS IN THE BODY

DIGESTIVE SYSTEM

BIOLOGY BOOKS FOR KIDS | Children's Biology Books

Speedy Publishing LLC
40 E. Main St. #1156
Newark, DE 19711
www.speedypublishing.com

Copyright © 2017

All Rights reserved. No part of this book may be reproduced or used in any way or form or by any means whether electronic or mechanical, this means that you cannot record or photocopy any material ideas or tips that are provided in this book.

The human body requires food for energy, minerals, and vitamins. We must first, however, break down the food into substances that the many cells and organs can use. This is what the digestive system does. In this book, you will learn about the digestive system and how it works with the other systems for survival of our body.

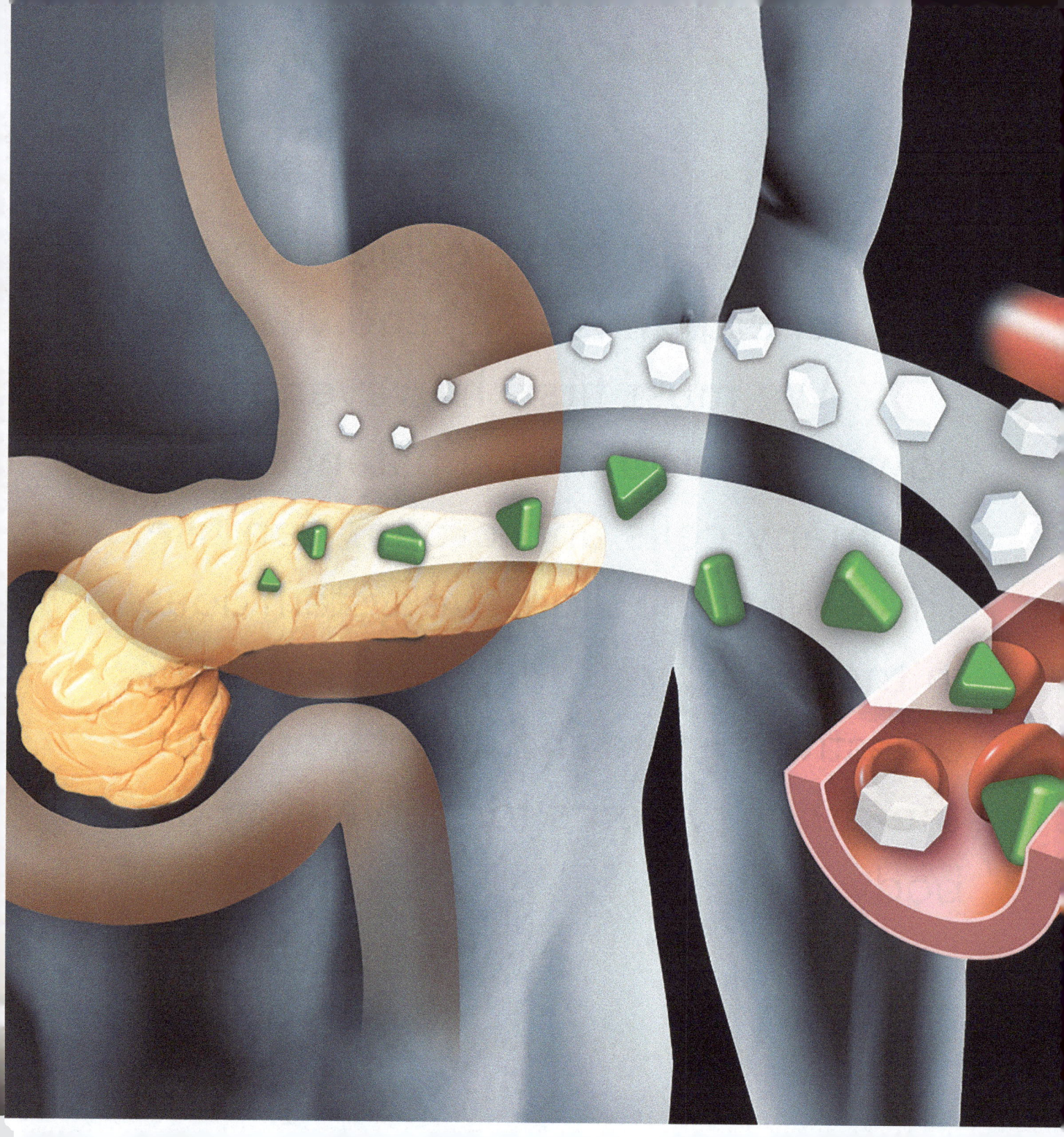

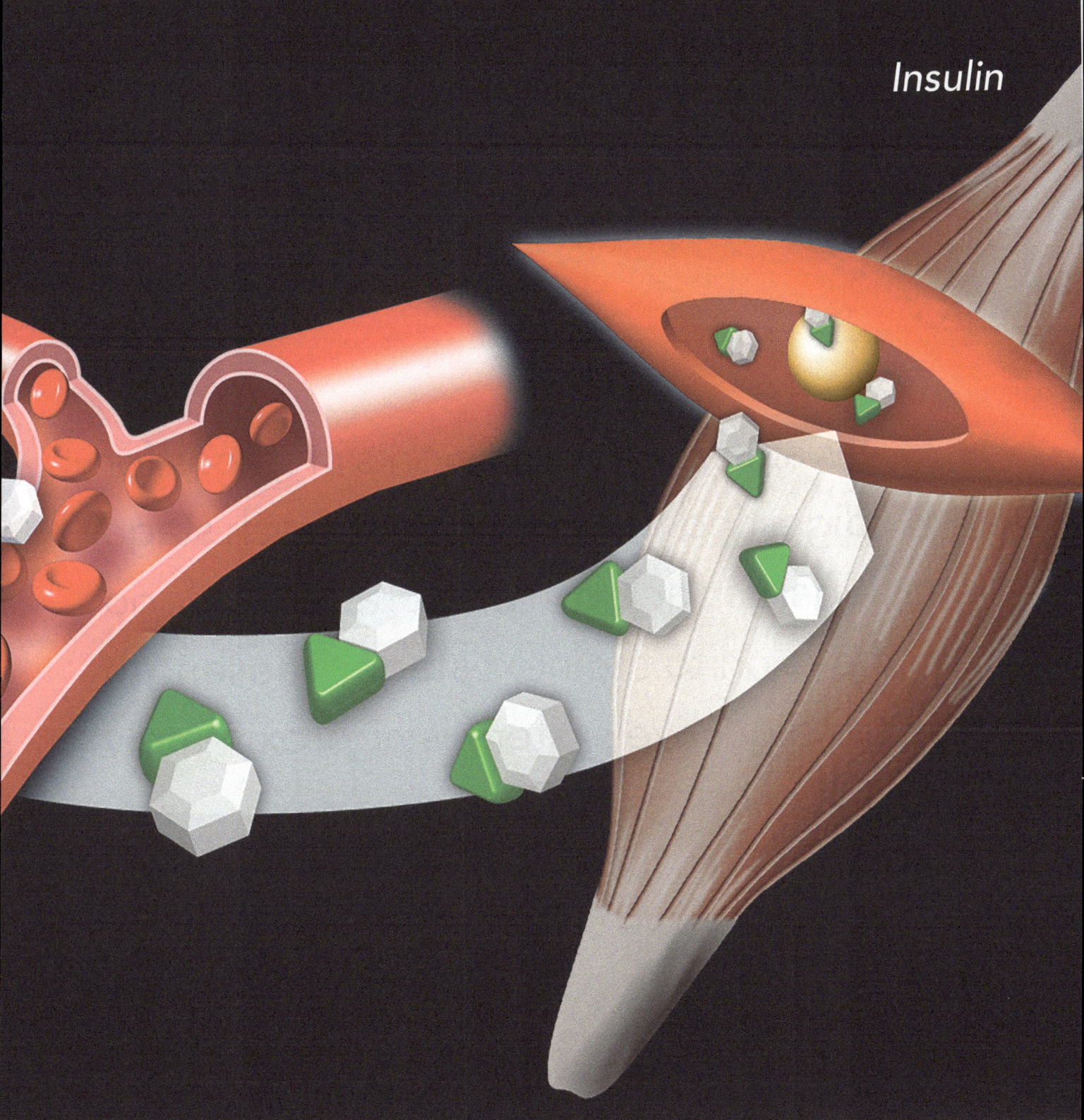

Insulin

THE DIGESTIVE SYSTEM

This amazing system works in stages for digesting the food we eat. Each stage has a particular job in preparation for food to move on to the next stage. The length of the digestive system is approximately 20 – 30 feet!

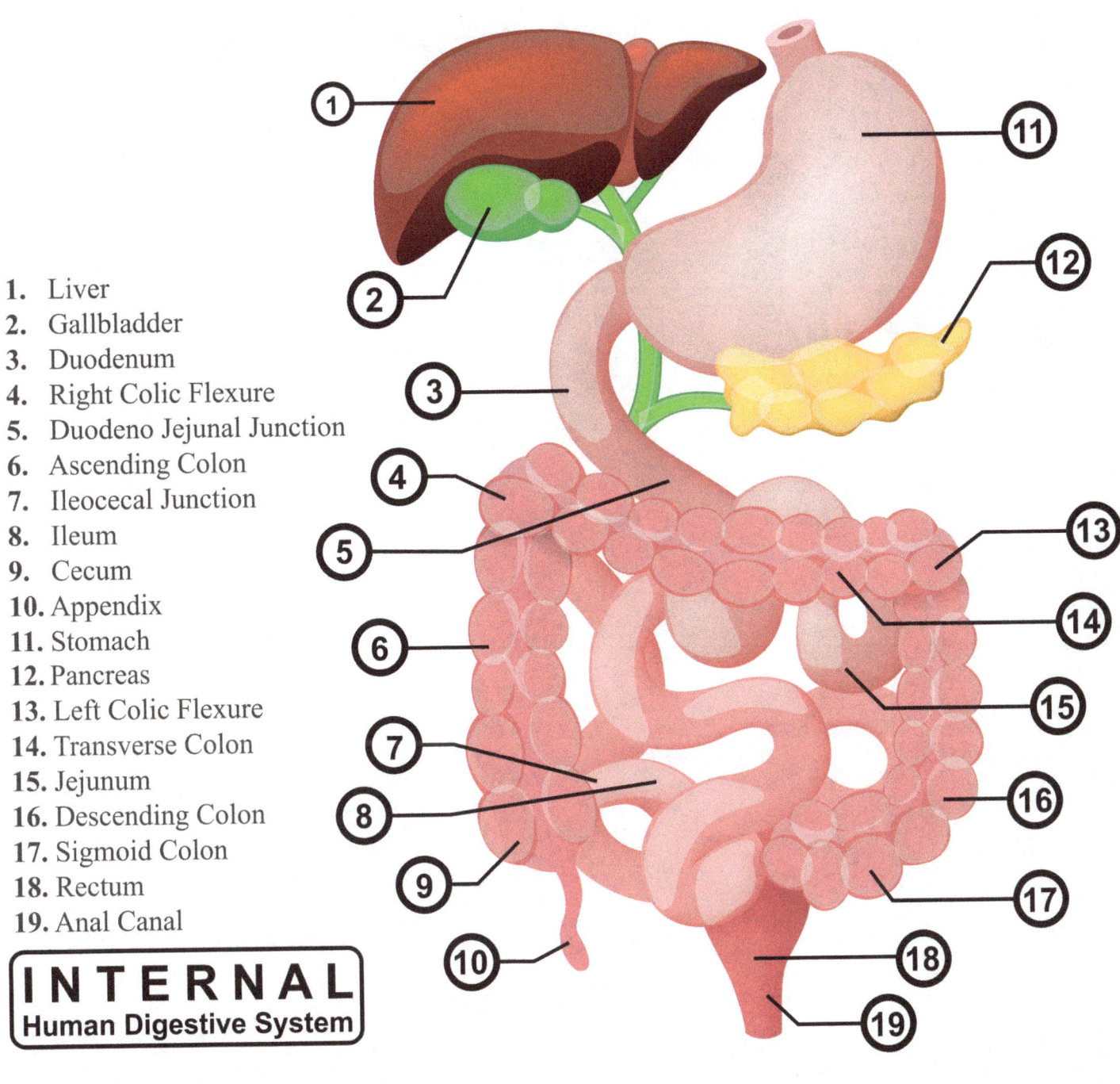

1. Liver
2. Gallbladder
3. Duodenum
4. Right Colic Flexure
5. Duodeno Jejunal Junction
6. Ascending Colon
7. Ileocecal Junction
8. Ileum
9. Cecum
10. Appendix
11. Stomach
12. Pancreas
13. Left Colic Flexure
14. Transverse Colon
15. Jejunum
16. Descending Colon
17. Sigmoid Colon
18. Rectum
19. Anal Canal

INTERNAL Human Digestive System

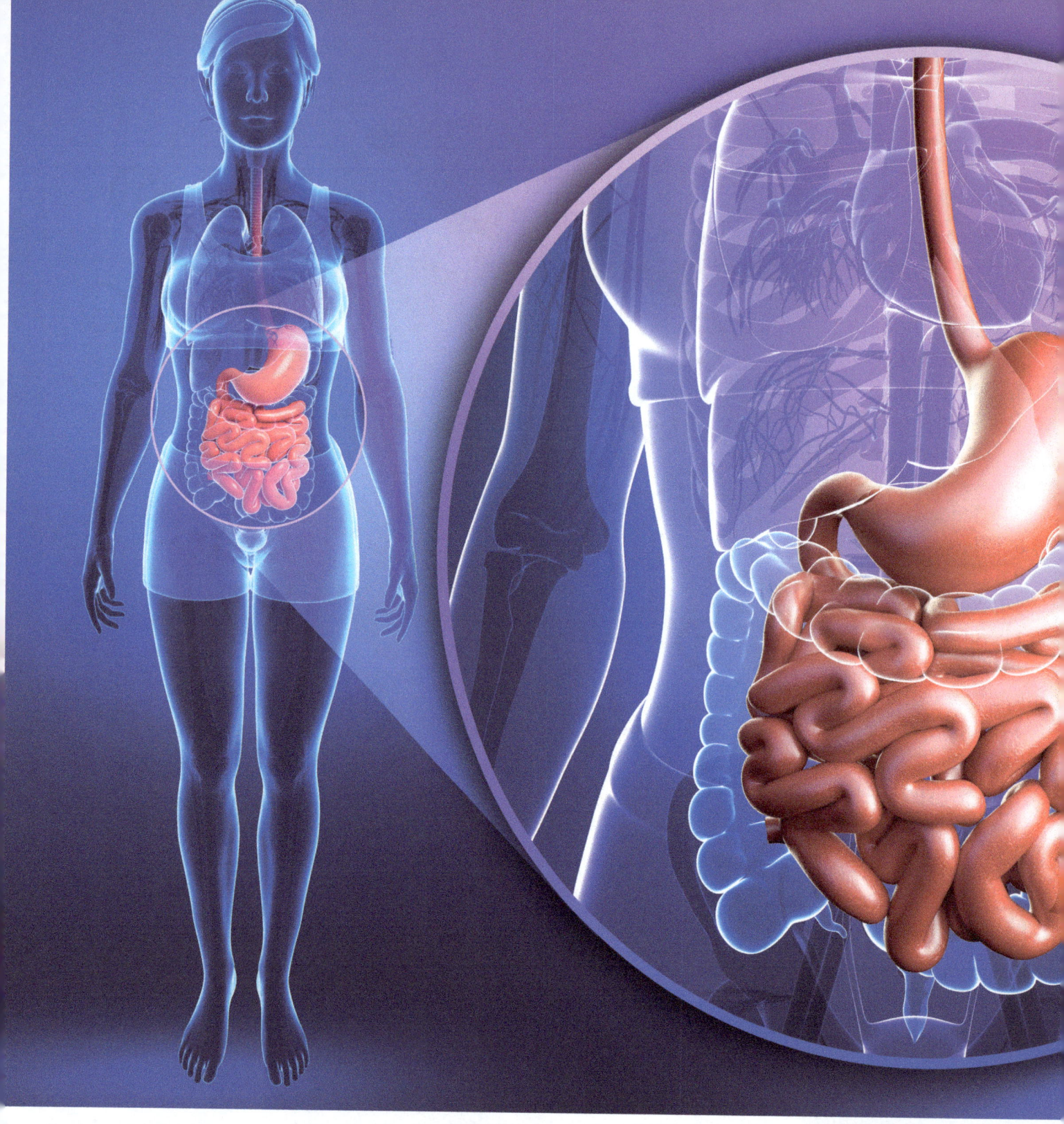

The Five Key Stages of Our Digestive System:

1. Chewing is the first step of our digestive system. As we chew food, we break the bigger pieces into smaller pieces so they are easier to swallow and digest. Additionally, saliva not only wets your mouth, it contains certain enzymes that start breaking down starchy foods such as bread and potatoes as you chew.

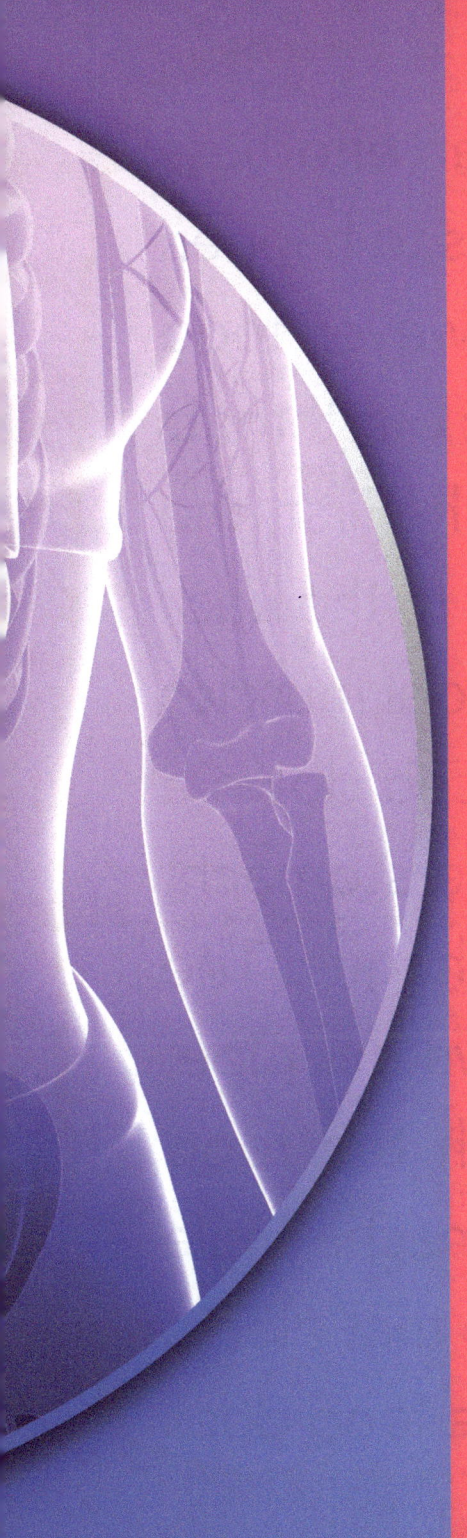

Small intestine Anatomy of Female.

2. Swallowing might seem like an effortless process to us, and it just seems to happen without thinking about it. However, food does not simply fall down into our throats and then onto to our stomach. First, the tongue works in pushing food to the back of the throat. Then, using special muscles in the throat, the food is forced down a long tube which leads to the stomach, which is known as the esophagus. The food does not simply fall down this pipe, there are muscles that push the food down until it reaches the stomach. While this is occurring, there is a flap that blocks the windpipe to make sure the food does

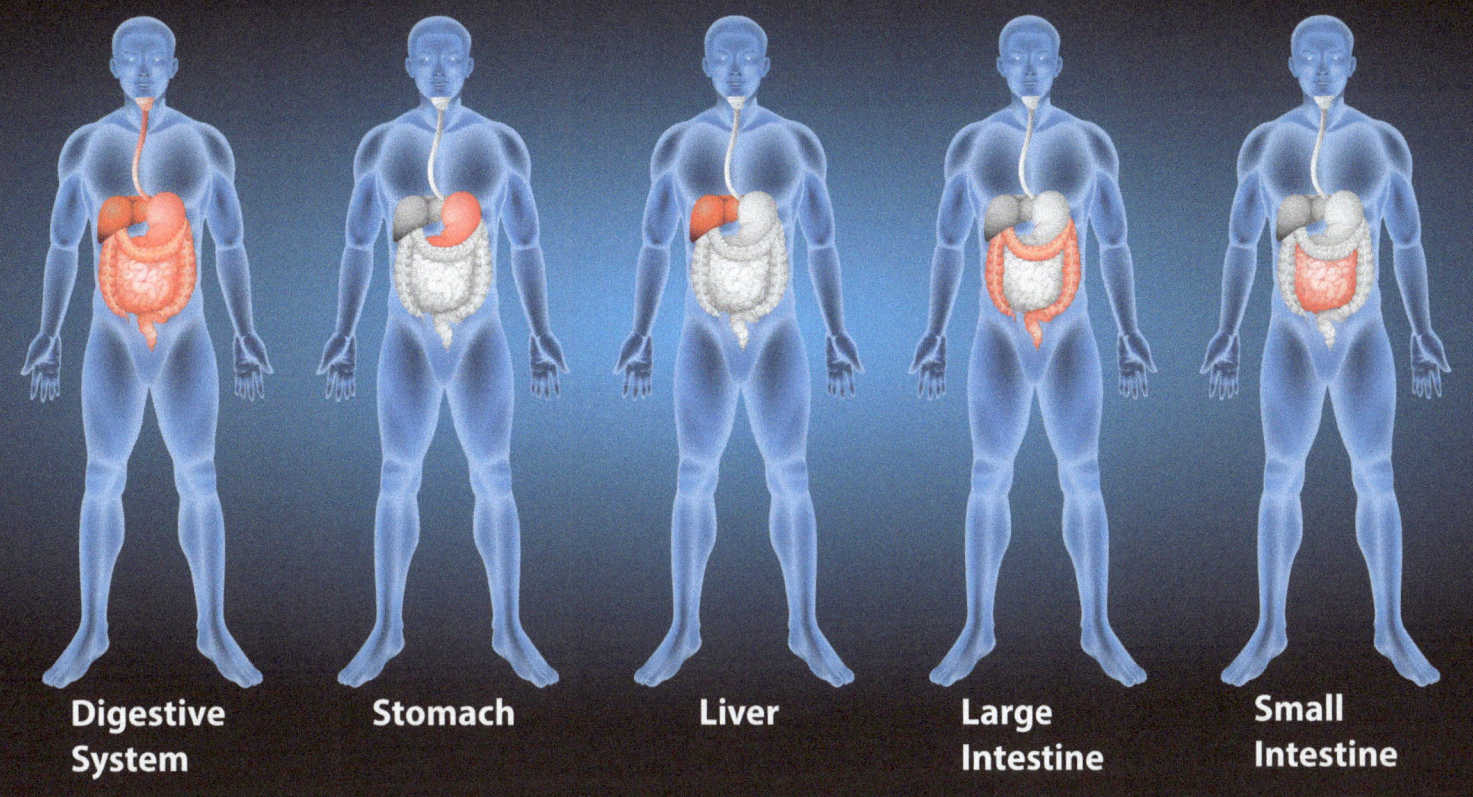

not go down the wrong way. This is referred to as *"going down the wrong way"* and it can cause choking. This flap is known as the epiglottis and, fortunately, it works automatically.

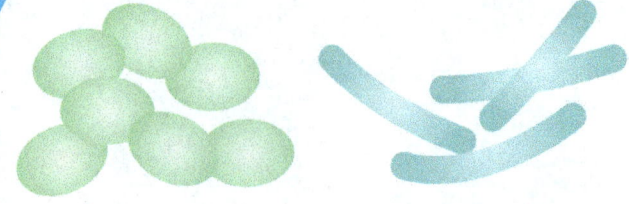
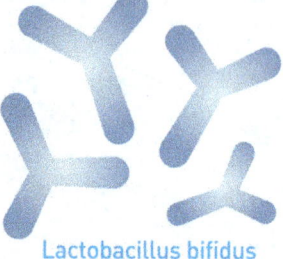
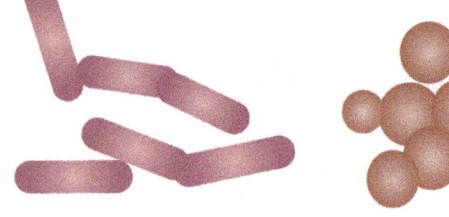
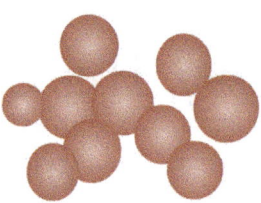
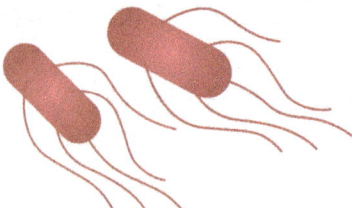
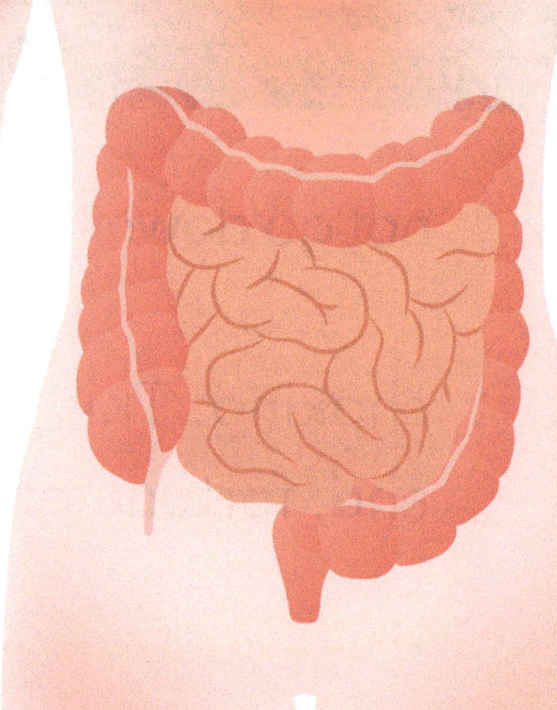

3. The stomach is the next stage. The food we eat will hang out for approximately four hours in the stomach. As it sits there, additional enzymes work on it to break down things such as protein for use throughout the body. The stomach also kills bad bacteria so that we don't become ill.

Good Bacteria and Bad Bacteria in the Gut.

4. The first section of our small intestine works alongside the juices received from the liver and pancreas and continues breaking down the food we ate. The second section is where food is absorbed into the body through blood flow.

5. The final stage is known as the large intestine. Any food that our body cannot use or doesn't need is sent to the large intestine and then later leaves as waste.

Pancreas Cross Section.

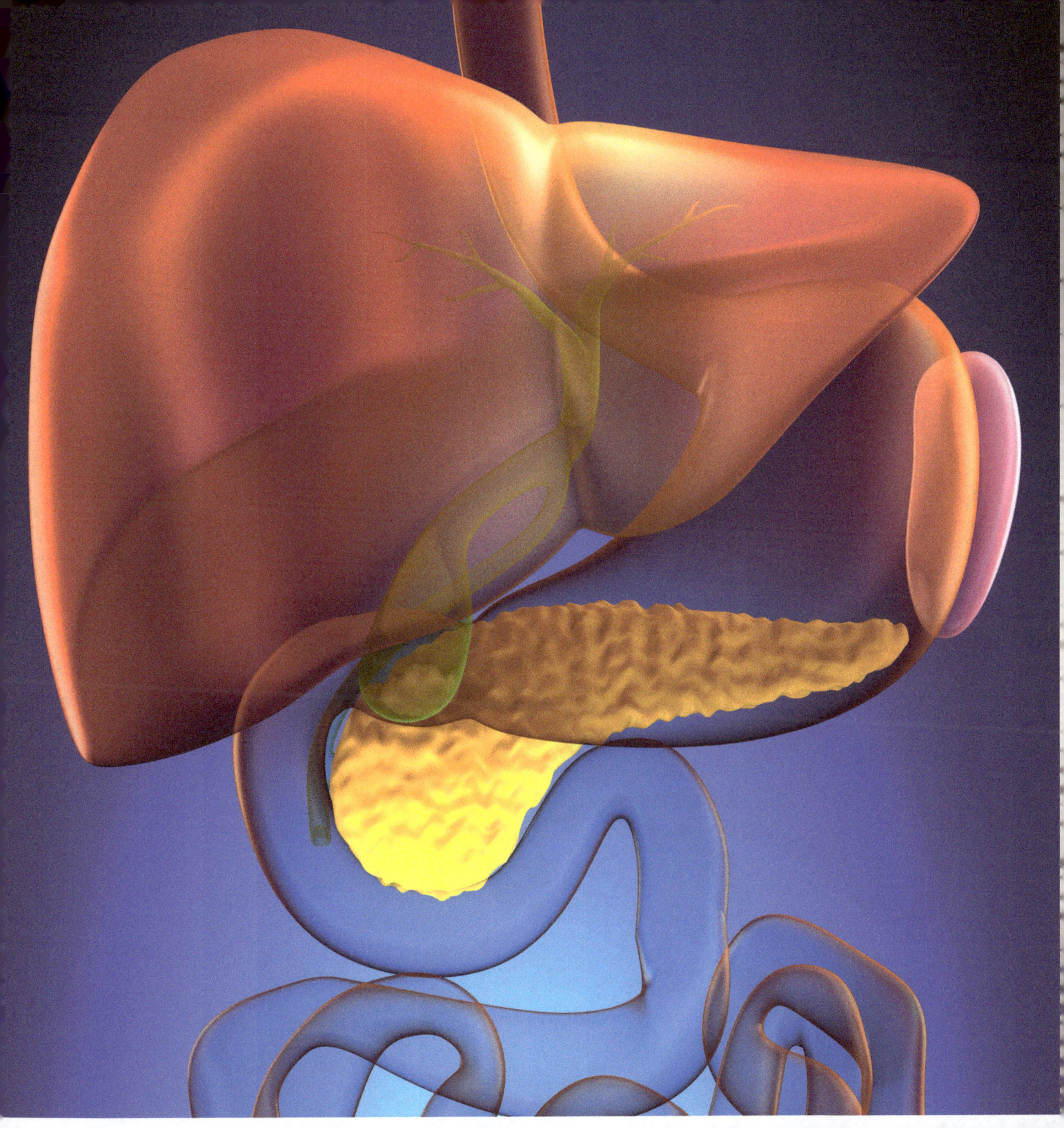

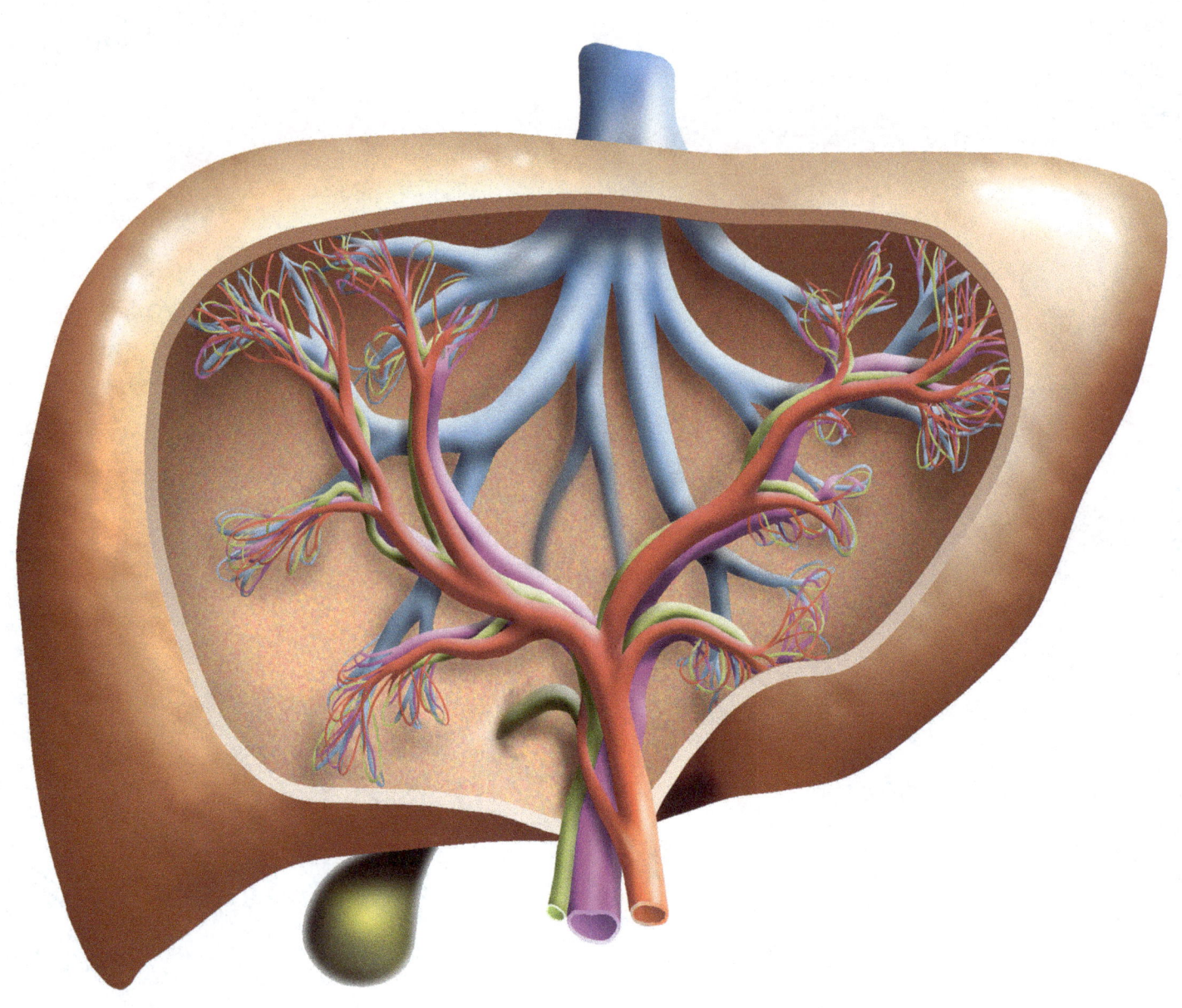

The Liver and Pancreas

These organs assist the digestive system quite a bit in moving things along, working with our small intestine. Bile, which is provided by the liver and stored in our gall bladder, works in breaking the fat up into smaller pieces. The pancreas provides more enzymes to assist with digestion of all types of food. In addition, the liver processes the food that has been digested before its sent to different places throughout your body.

Human Liver.

What are Enzymes?

Enzymes are specific kinds of proteins. Similar to other proteins, they consist of strings of amino acids. The enzyme's function is decided by the amino acid sequence, the kind of amino acid, and the shape of its string.

Stomach, Gallbladder and Pancreas.

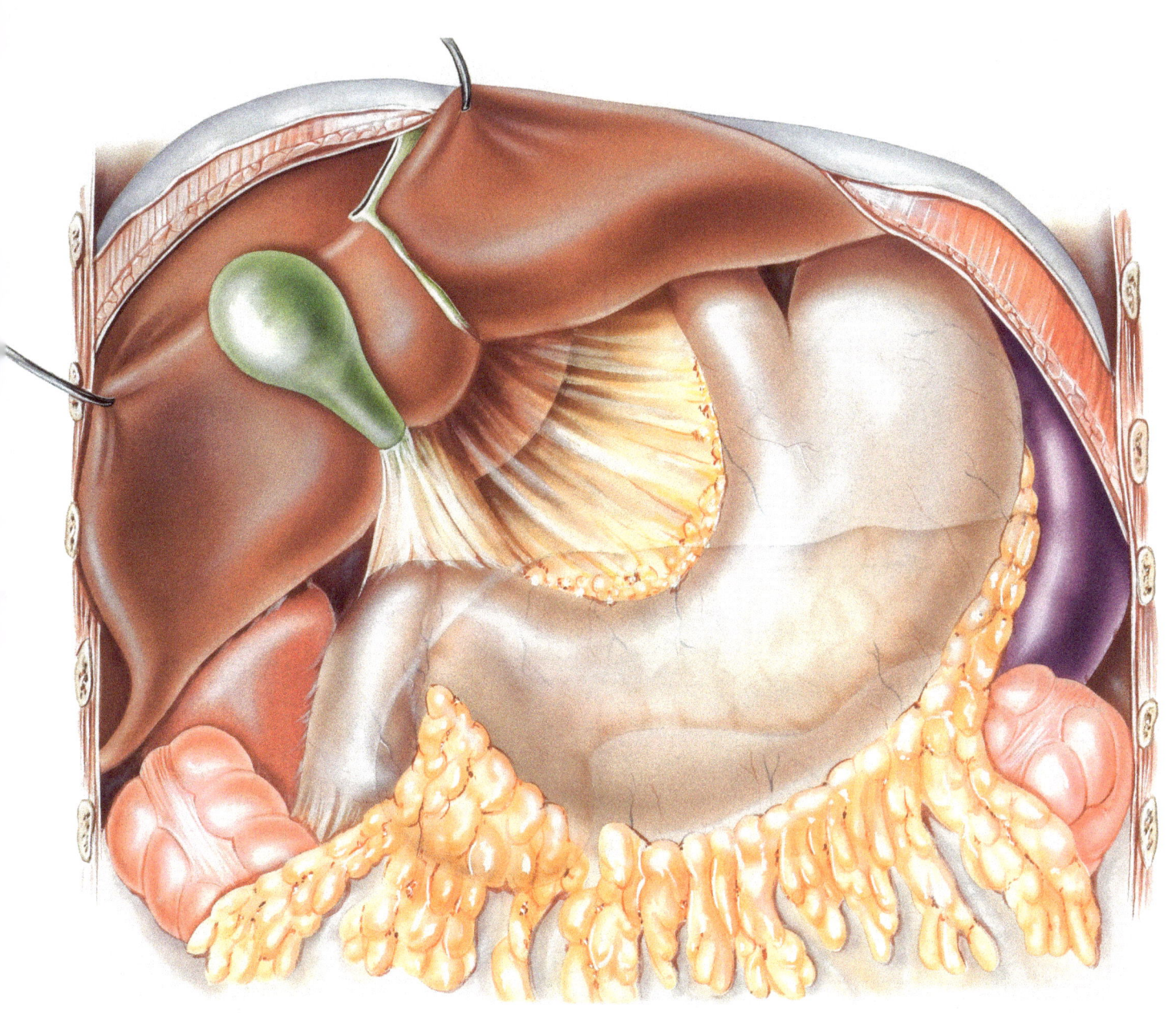

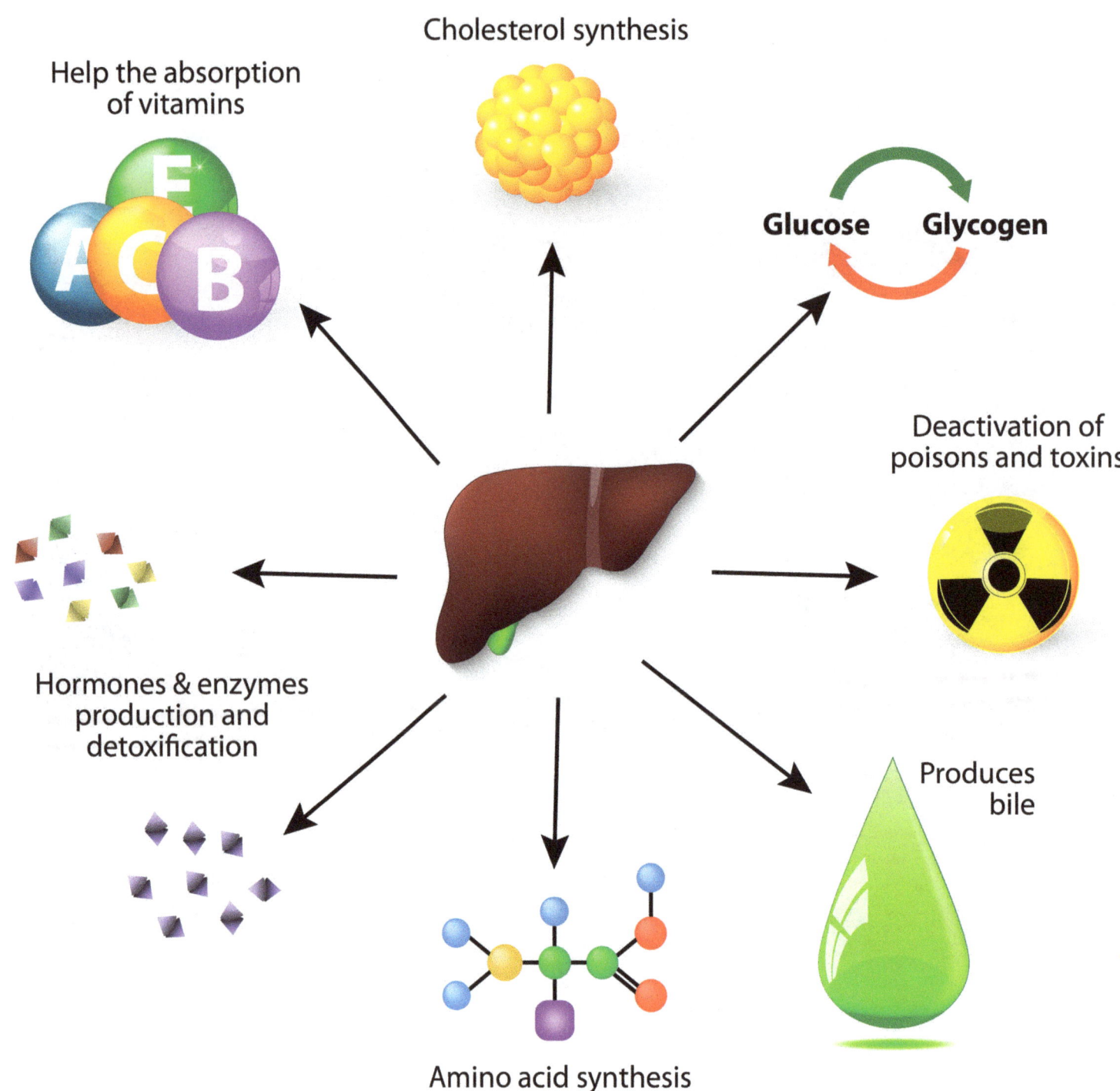

What is the Function of the Enzymes?

They are responsible for much of the work that takes place in cells. They act as a catalyst to produce and speed up chemical reactions. A cell will usually use an enzyme in order to speed up the process when it needs something done.

Liver Functions: Synthesis of protein, amino acid and cholesterol, deactivation of poisons and toxins, produces bile, help the absorption of vitamins, hormones & enzymes production and detoxification.

Enzymes are Specific

As discussed earlier, enzymes are quite specific, which means that each kind will only react with a certain type of substance. This is a very important function so that enzymes don't do something wrong and cause an incorrect chemical reaction.

Insulin, cells.

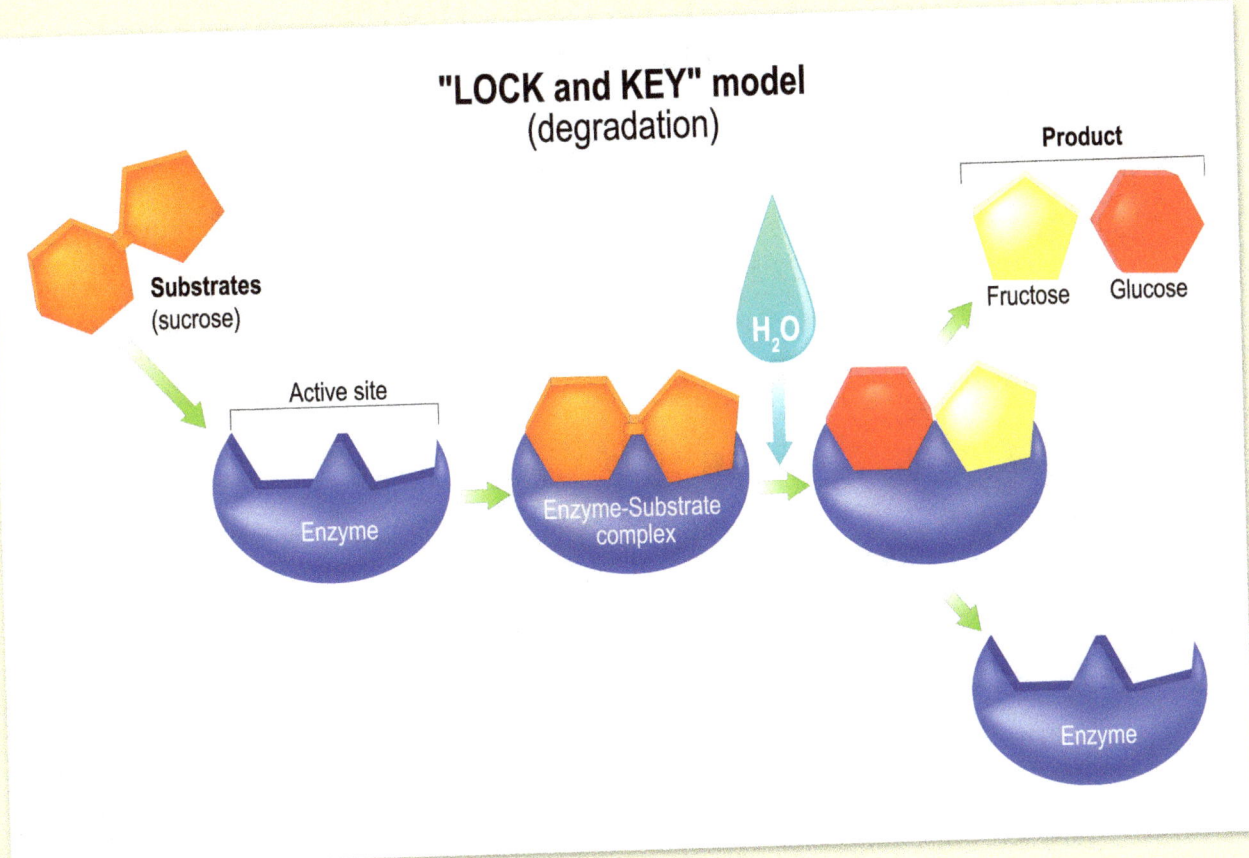

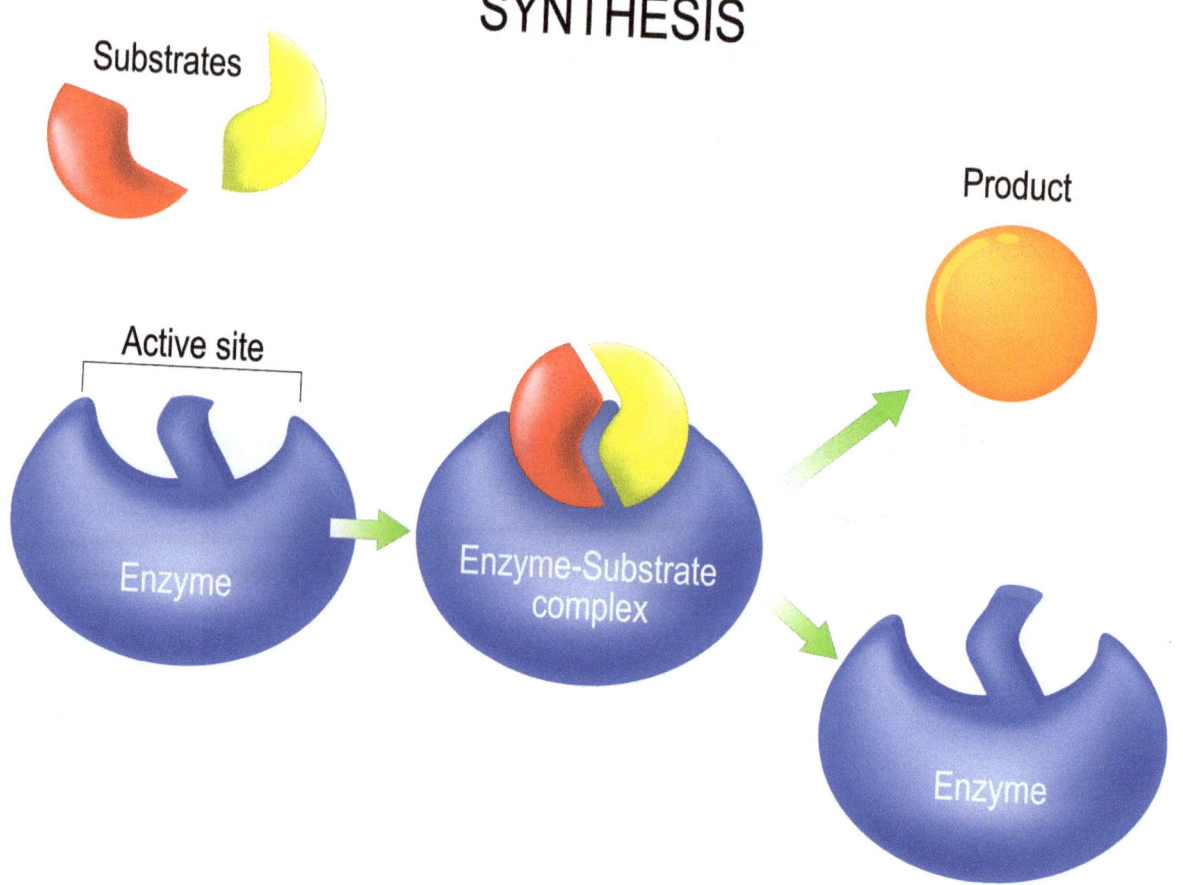

How Do Enzymes Work

There is a special pocket on the surface of the enzyme which is referred to as an *"active site"*. The molecule which they are supposed to reach with fits right in that pocket. The substance or molecule that reacts with the enzyme is known as the *"substrate"*.

The reaction occurring between the enzyme and the substrate occurs at the active site. Once the reaction is finished, the new substance or molecule is then released by the enzyme, and the new substance is known as the *"product"*.

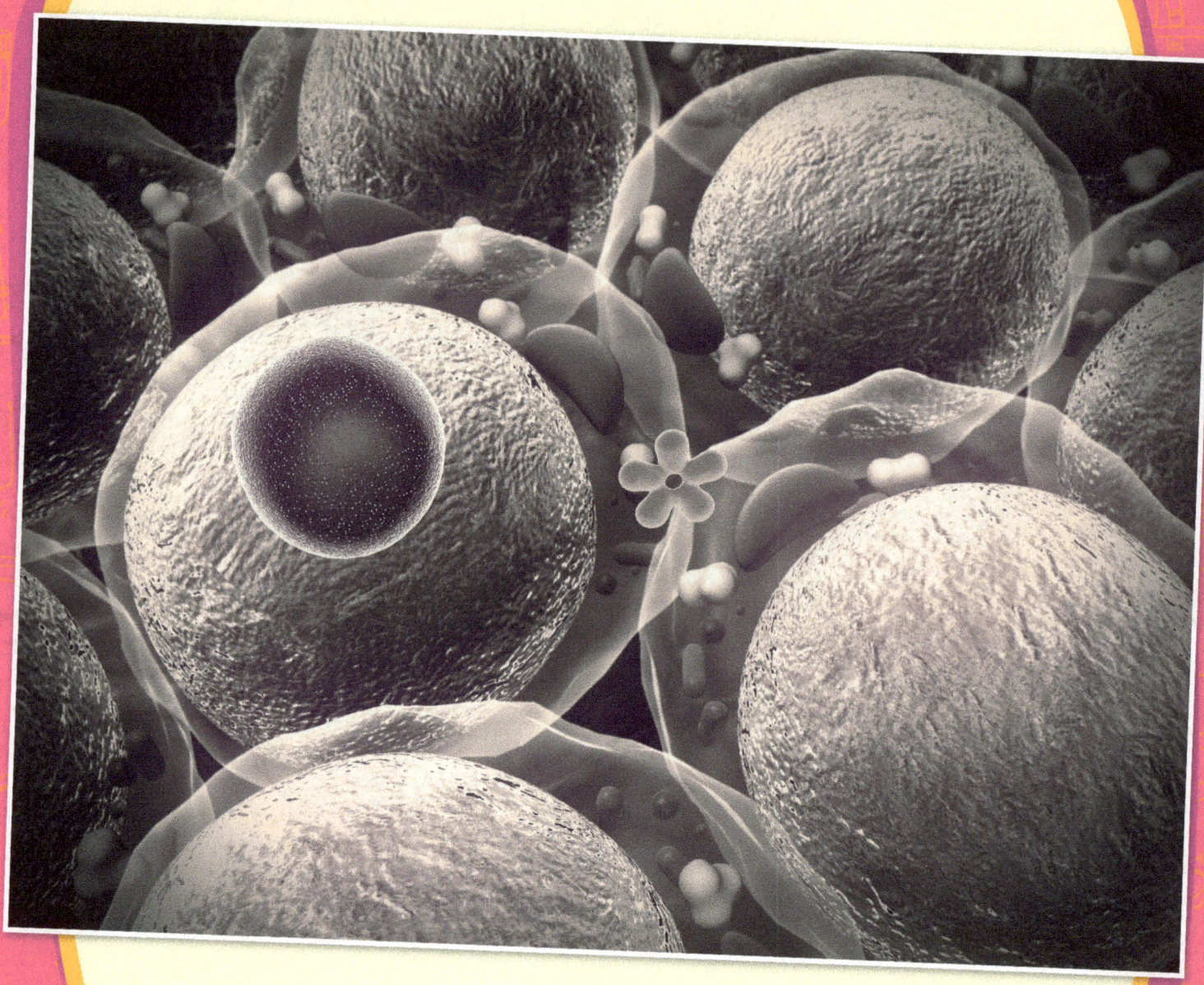

Things that Affect Enzyme Activity

The surrounding environment of the substrate and enzyme can have an effect on the speed of the reaction. In certain cases, the environment may cause it to quit working or possibly unravel. Once an enzyme quits working it is referred to as *"denatured"*. Here is a list of some of the things that might affect enzyme activity.

Mitochondria and Proteins.

- Temperature might affect the rate of reaction. As the temperature becomes warmer, the reaction becomes quicker. At some point, however, the temperature gets so hot that it becomes denatured and quits working.

Enzyme Catalase, a very important antioxidant in organisms.

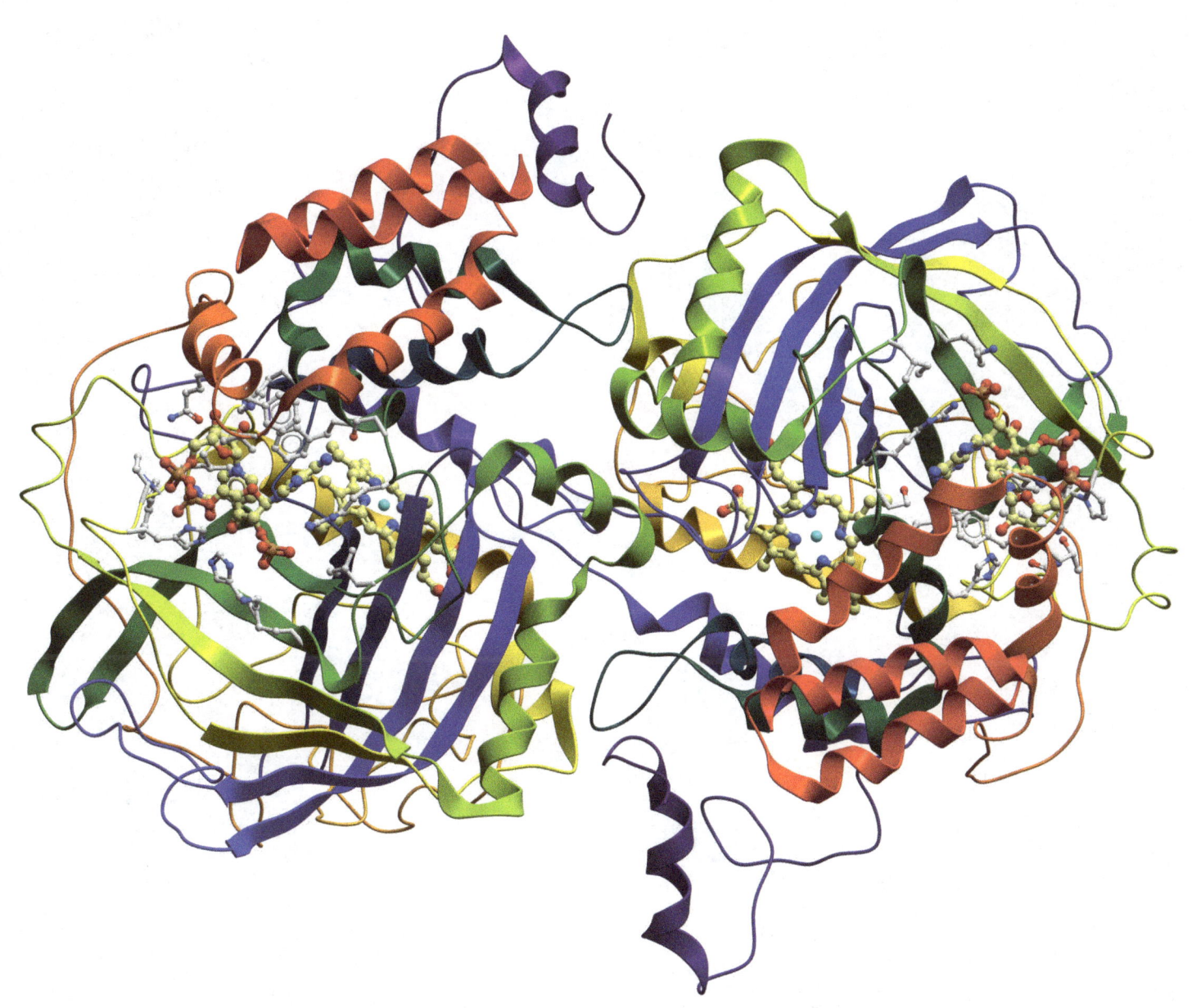

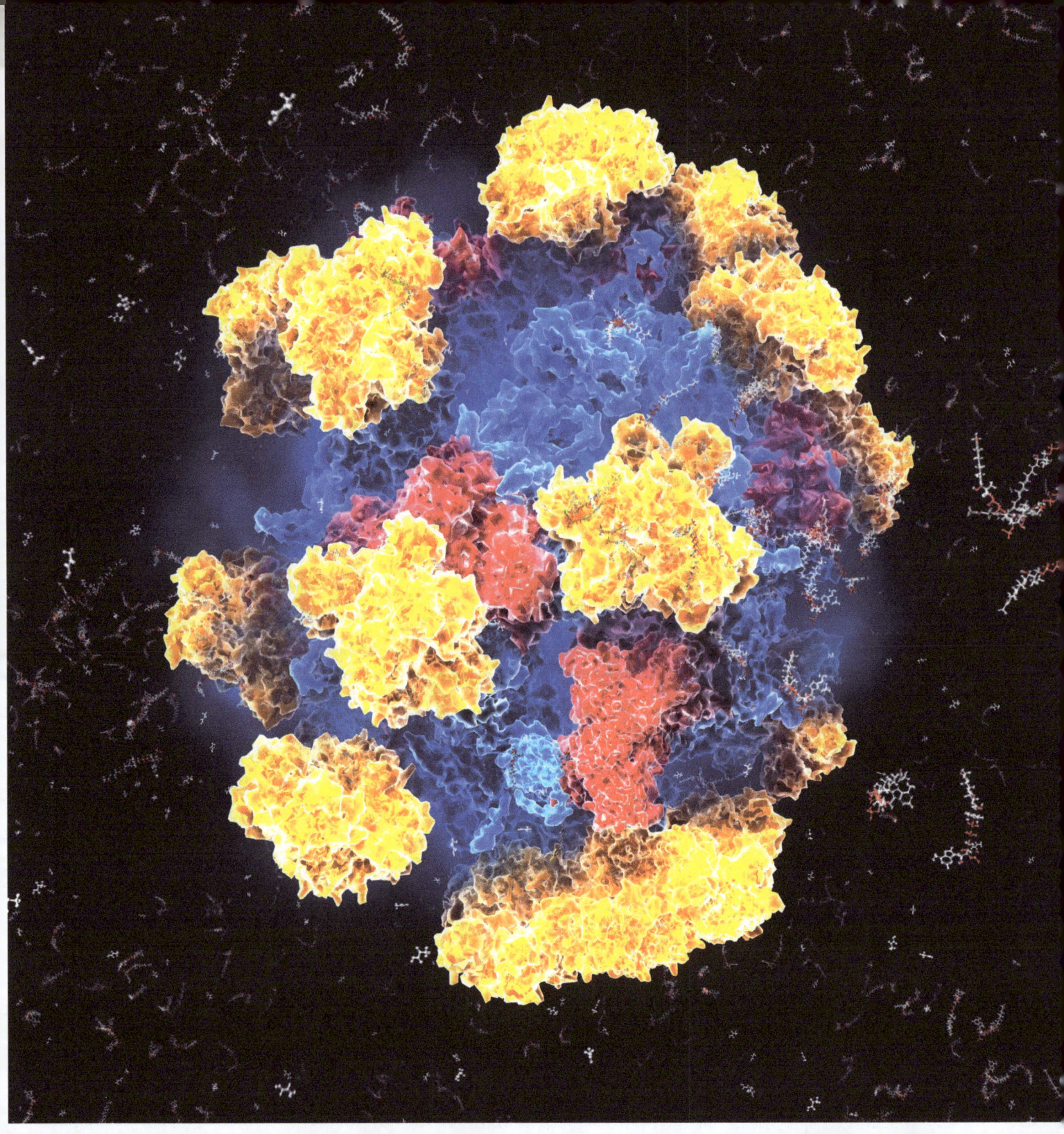

- In several cases, the level of the pH, or acidity, of the environment surrounding the enzyme and substrate may affect the rate of reaction. Any extreme pH (low or high) typically will slow down the reaction or possibly stop it altogether.

- Concentration of the enzyme can also affect the activity. If the concentration of the enzyme or substrate is higher, the reaction rate will be increased.

Enzyme in Action.

- Inhibitors are the molecules made specifically to stop enzyme activity. They might simply slow the reaction down, or stop it completely. Some of them bond along with the enzyme and cause it to change its shape and not be able to work correctly. The activator is the opposite of the inhibitor and can assist in speeding up the reaction.

Intestine Lining and Villi.

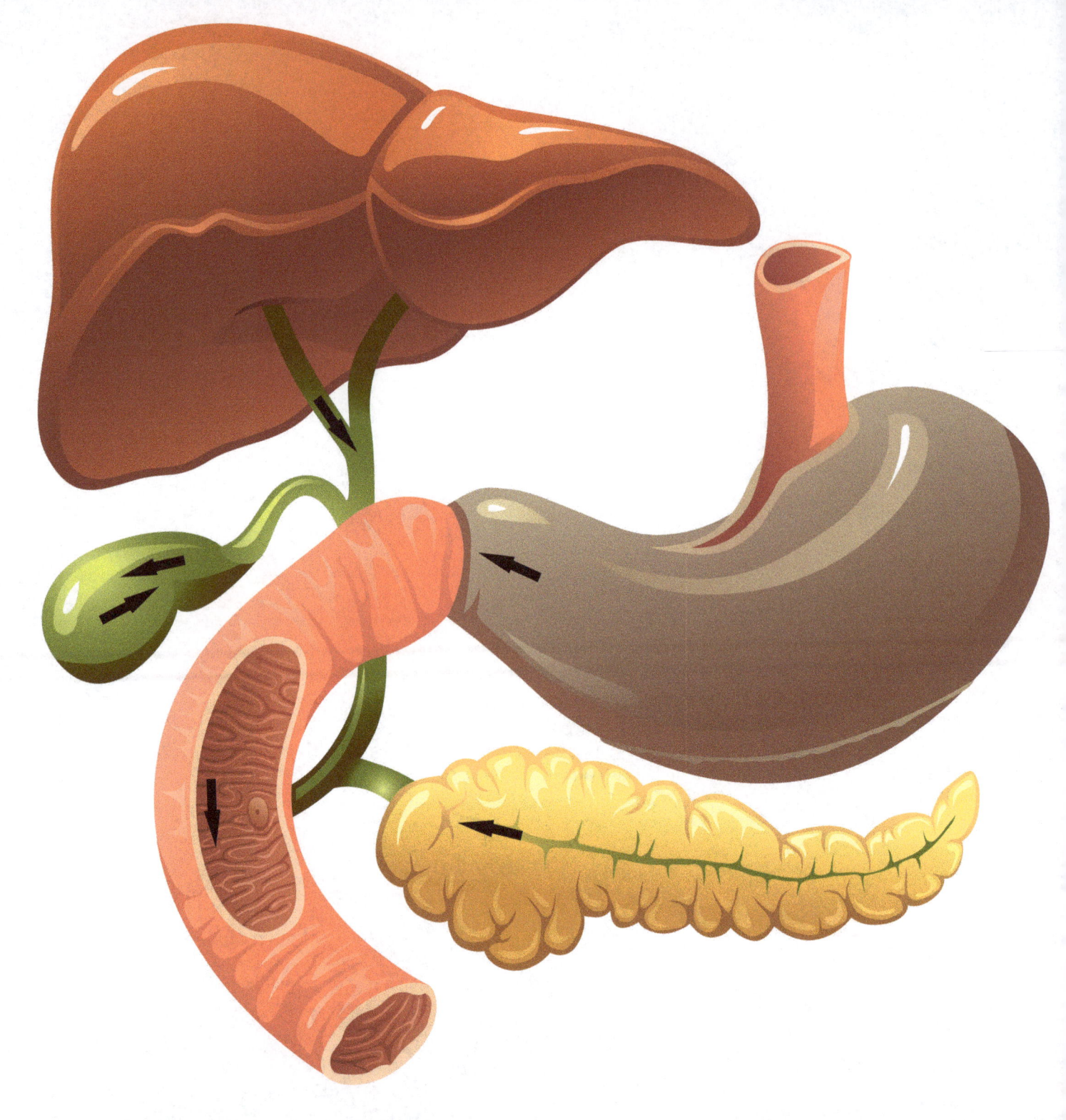

What is an Organ?

A group of tissues within a living organism having a specific function and form is known as an organ.

Organs of the Digestive System.

Organ Systems

Organs are grouped into organ systems and each system performs a certain task. There are ten major systems in most animals:

- **NERVOUS SYSTEM** - The nervous system carries messages from our brain to the various parts of our body, and includes the brain, nerves, and spinal cord.

Nervous System.

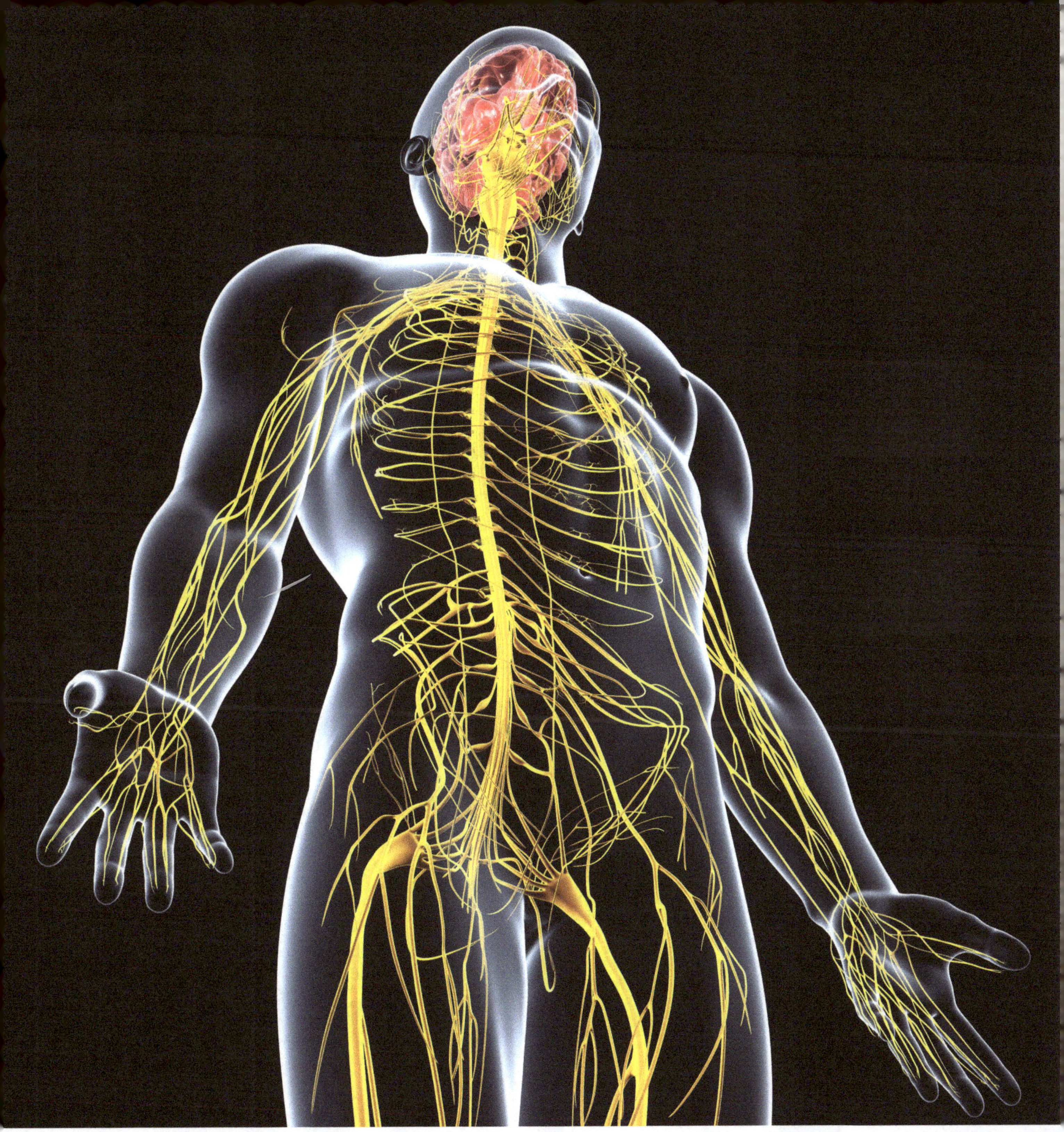

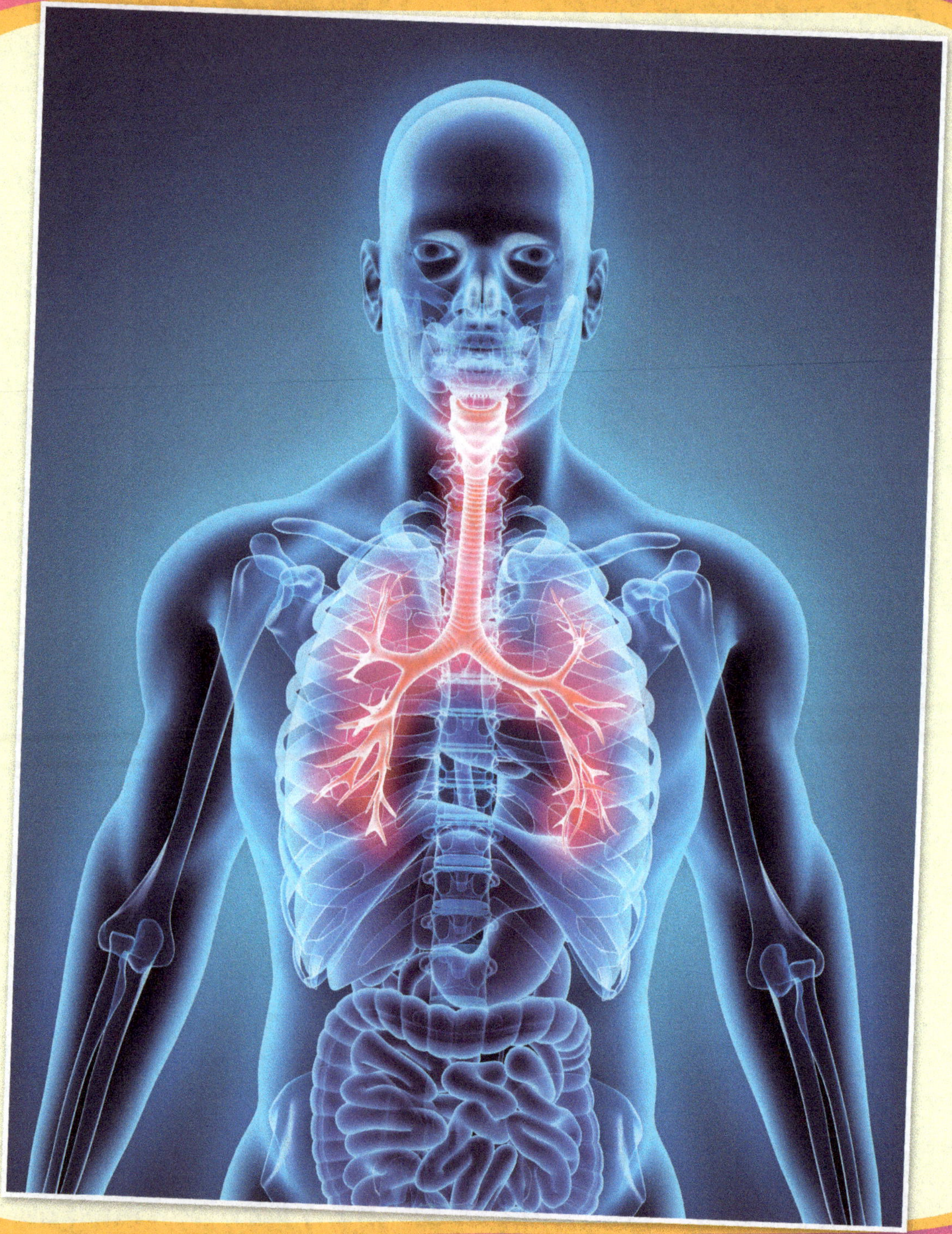

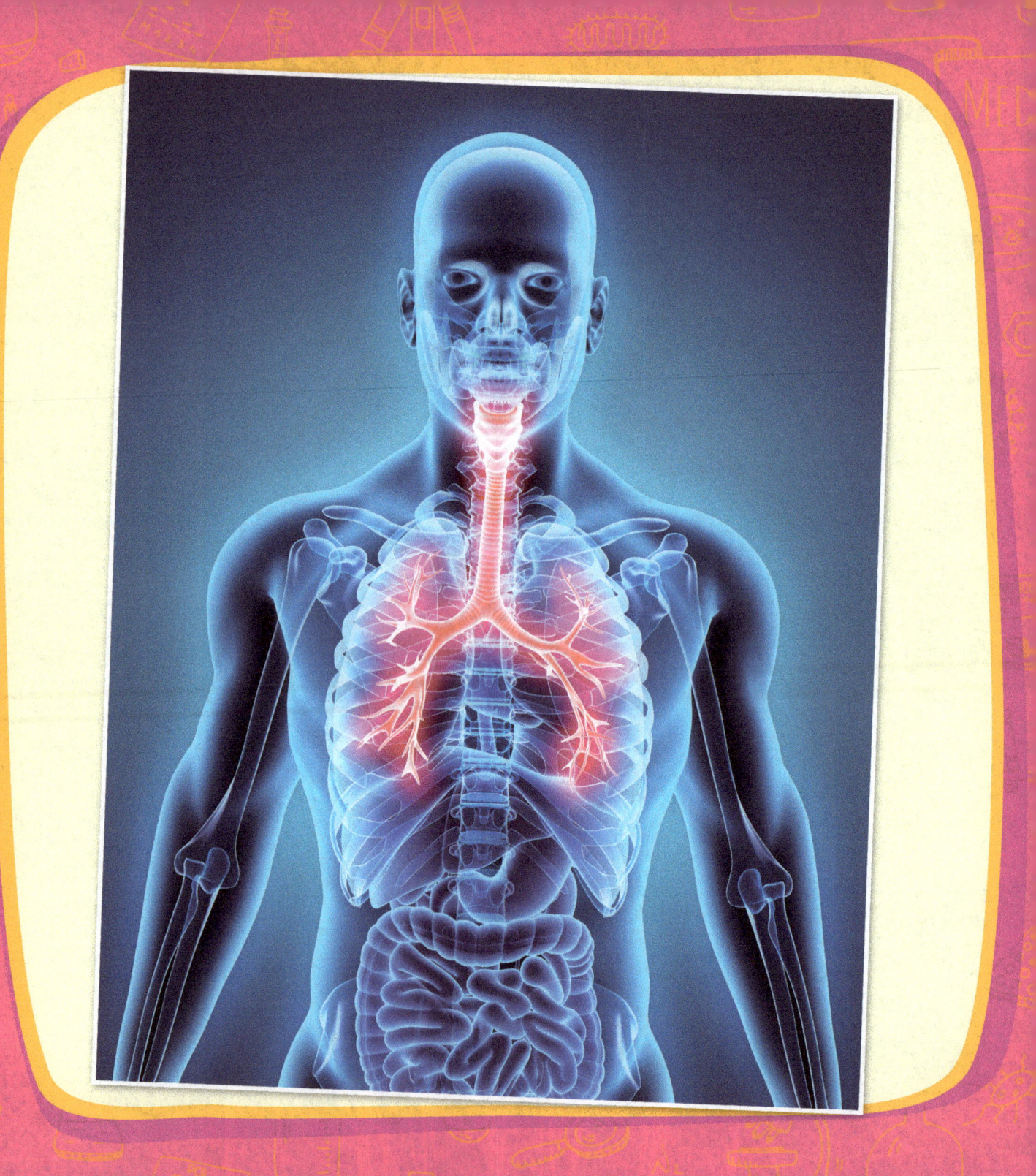

- **RESPIRATORY SYSTEM** - The respiratory system, consisting of the airways, larynx, and lungs, is responsible for our breathing by transferring oxygen to the blood stream and removing the carbon dioxide.

- **CARDIOVASCULAR / CIRCULATORY SYSTEM** - The cardiovascular / circulatory system is responsible for carrying the blood throughout our body to assist in providing nutrients to various organs. It includes the blood vessels, heart, and blood.

Larynx Trachea Bronchi.

- **DIGESTIVE SYSTEM** - As discussed earlier, this system is responsible for processing the food and sending energy and nutrients to the rest of the body. Organs included in the digestive system are the gallbladder, stomach, pancreas, lives, and intestines.

Human Male Digestive System.

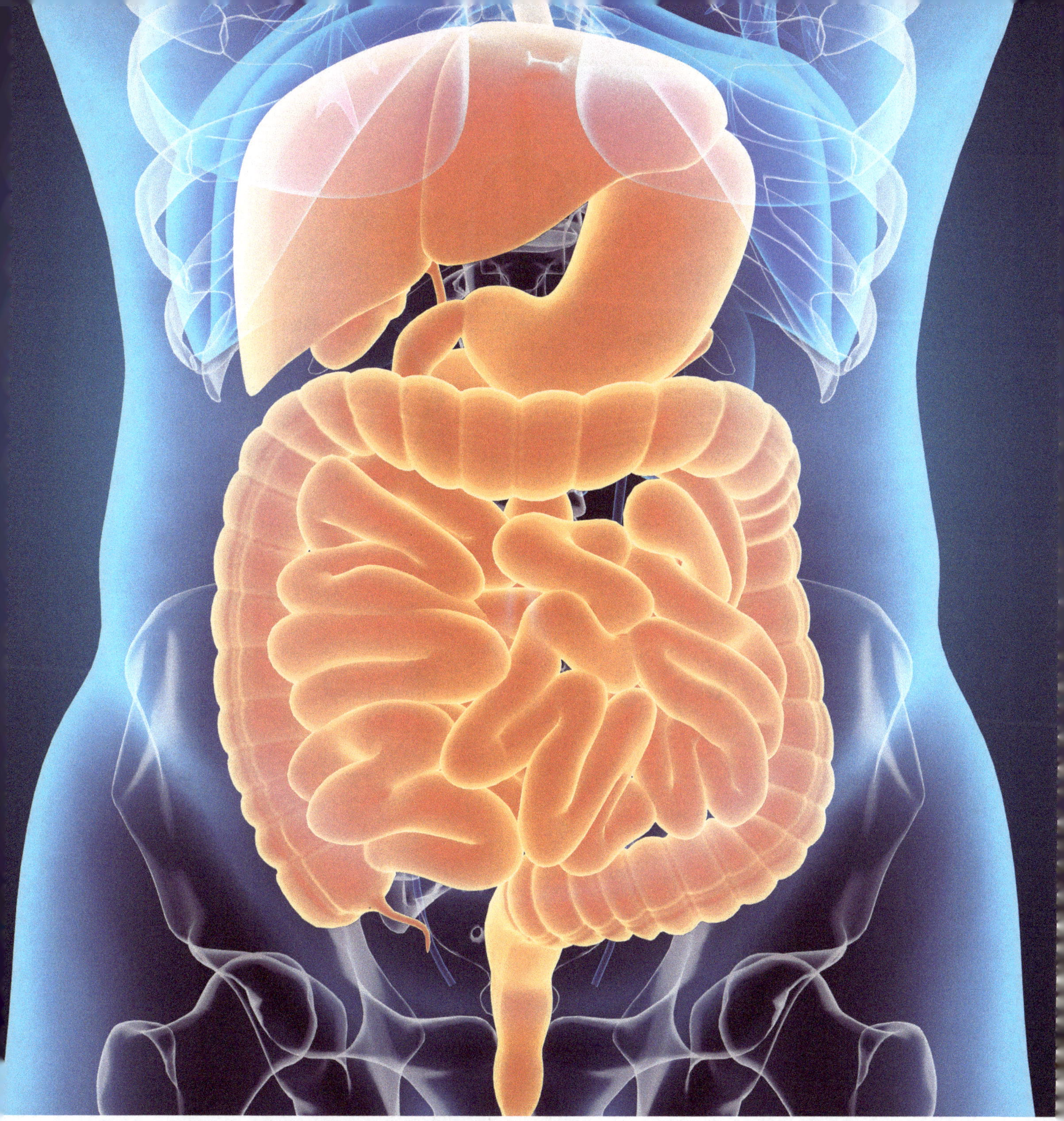

ENDOCRINE SYSTEM

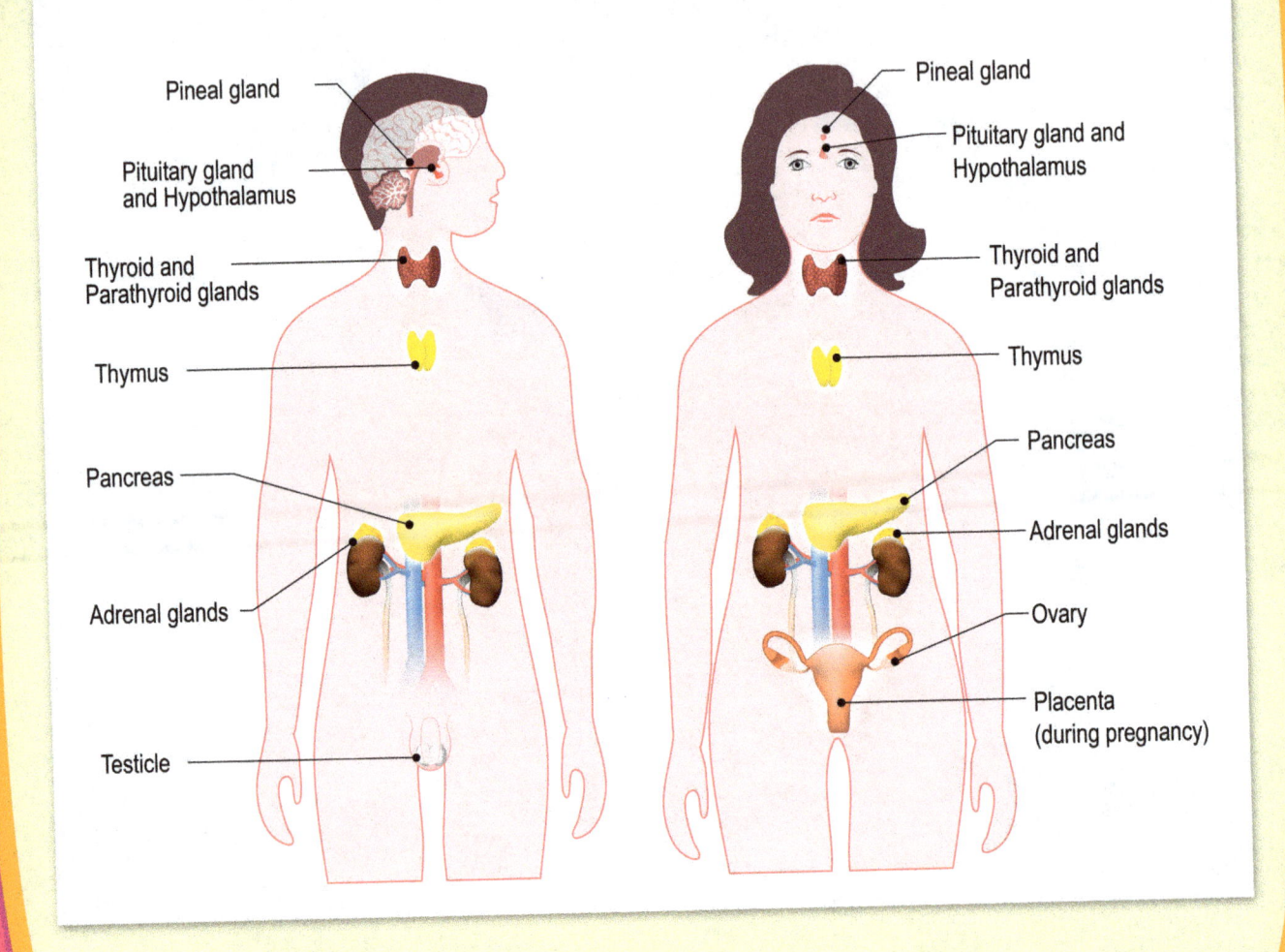

- Pineal gland
- Pituitary gland and Hypothalamus
- Thyroid and Parathyroid glands
- Thymus
- Pancreas
- Adrenal glands
- Testicle

- Pineal gland
- Pituitary gland and Hypothalamus
- Thyroid and Parathyroid glands
- Thymus
- Pancreas
- Adrenal glands
- Ovary
- Placenta (during pregnancy)

- **ENDOCRINE SYSTEM** - The endocrine system utilizes hormones for regulation of several functions through the body including mood, growth, reproduction, and metabolism. The major organs of the endocrine system are the thyroid, pituitary, and adrenal glands.

The Endocrine System.

- **EXCRETORY SYSTEM** - The excretory system works to eliminate food and toxins that your body does not need, using organs such as the bladder and kidneys.

- **INTEGUMENTARY SYSTEM** - The integumentary system protects our body from the world around us and includes skin, nails, and hair.

Types of Muscle Tissue

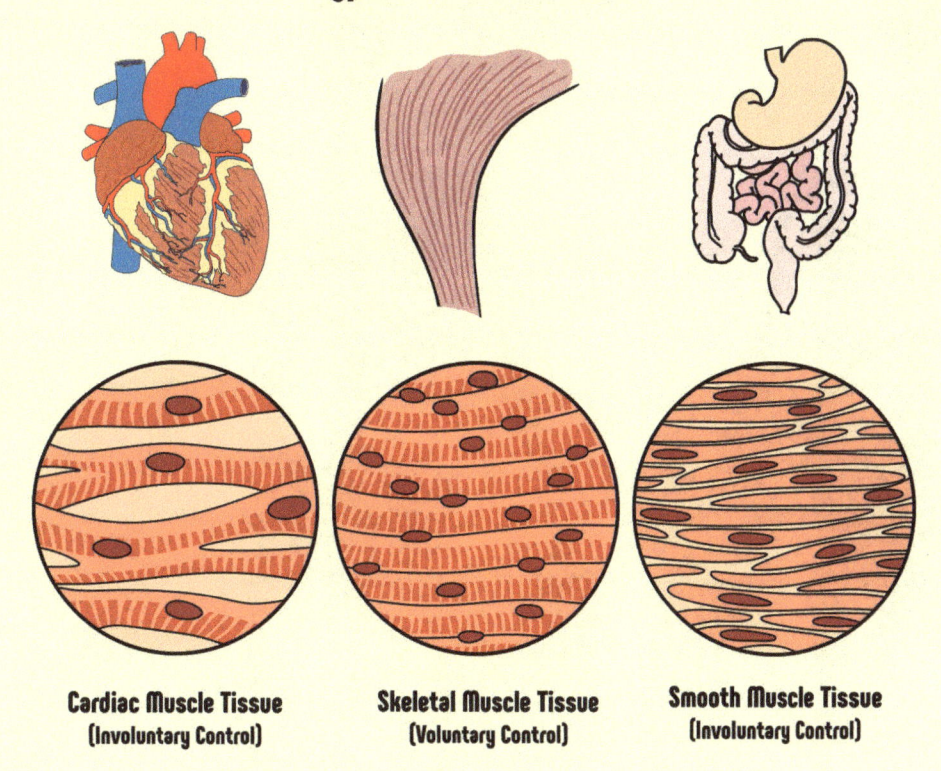

Cardiac Muscle Tissue
(Involuntary Control)

Skeletal Muscle Tissue
(Voluntary Control)

Smooth Muscle Tissue
(Involuntary Control)

- **MUSCULAR SYSTEM** - The muscular system consists of all the muscles within our bodies and is controlled by the nervous system.

Types of Muscle Tissue of Human Body Diagram.

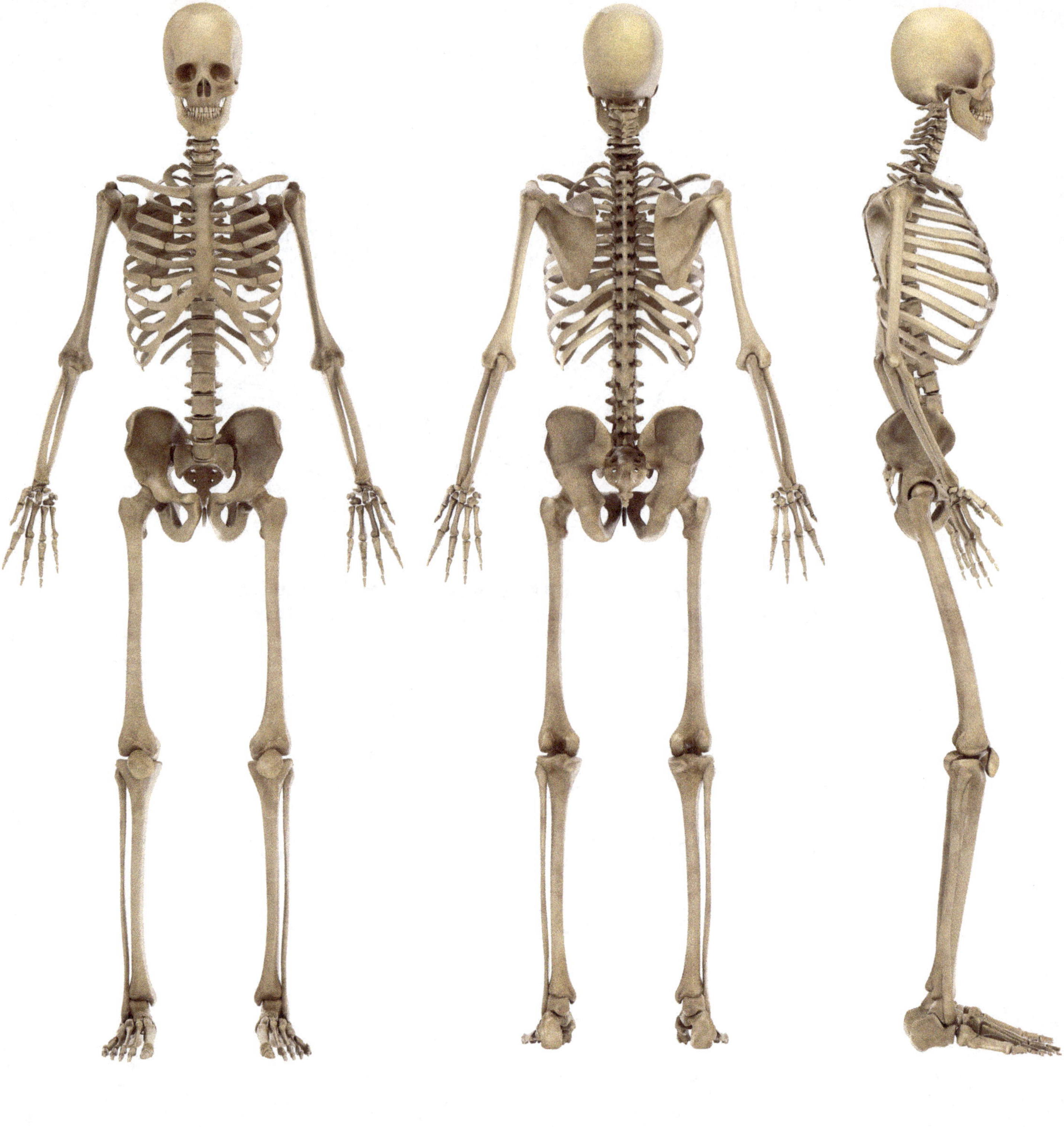

- **REPRODUCTIVE SYSTEM** - The reproductive system consists of the organs which are required for reproduction. Unlike the other systems, the reproductive system differs in females versus males.

- **SKELETAL SYSTEM** - The skeletal system supports and protects the remaining organ systems. It consists of ligaments, bones, cartilage, and tendons.

Skeleton

Major Organs

As seen in the long list of systems, the human body consists of many organs that all work together somehow in order to keep us alive. Below is a listing and quick description of some of the major organs.

- **BRAIN** - This is probably the most important organ in the human body. We use it to feel emotions, make decisions and control the rest of our body. It is surrounded by fluid and a thick skull.

Brain

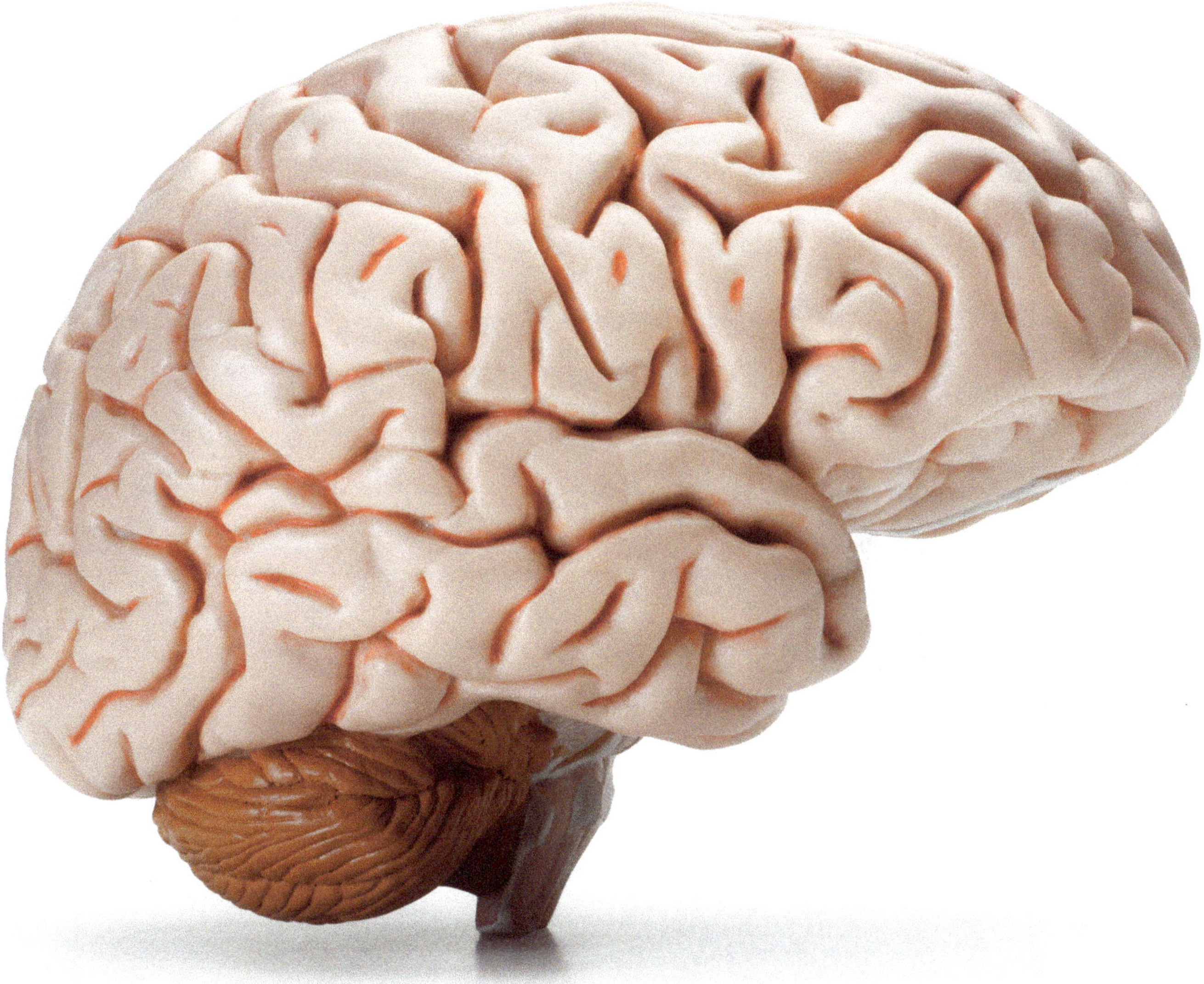

HUMAN LIVER STRUCTURE

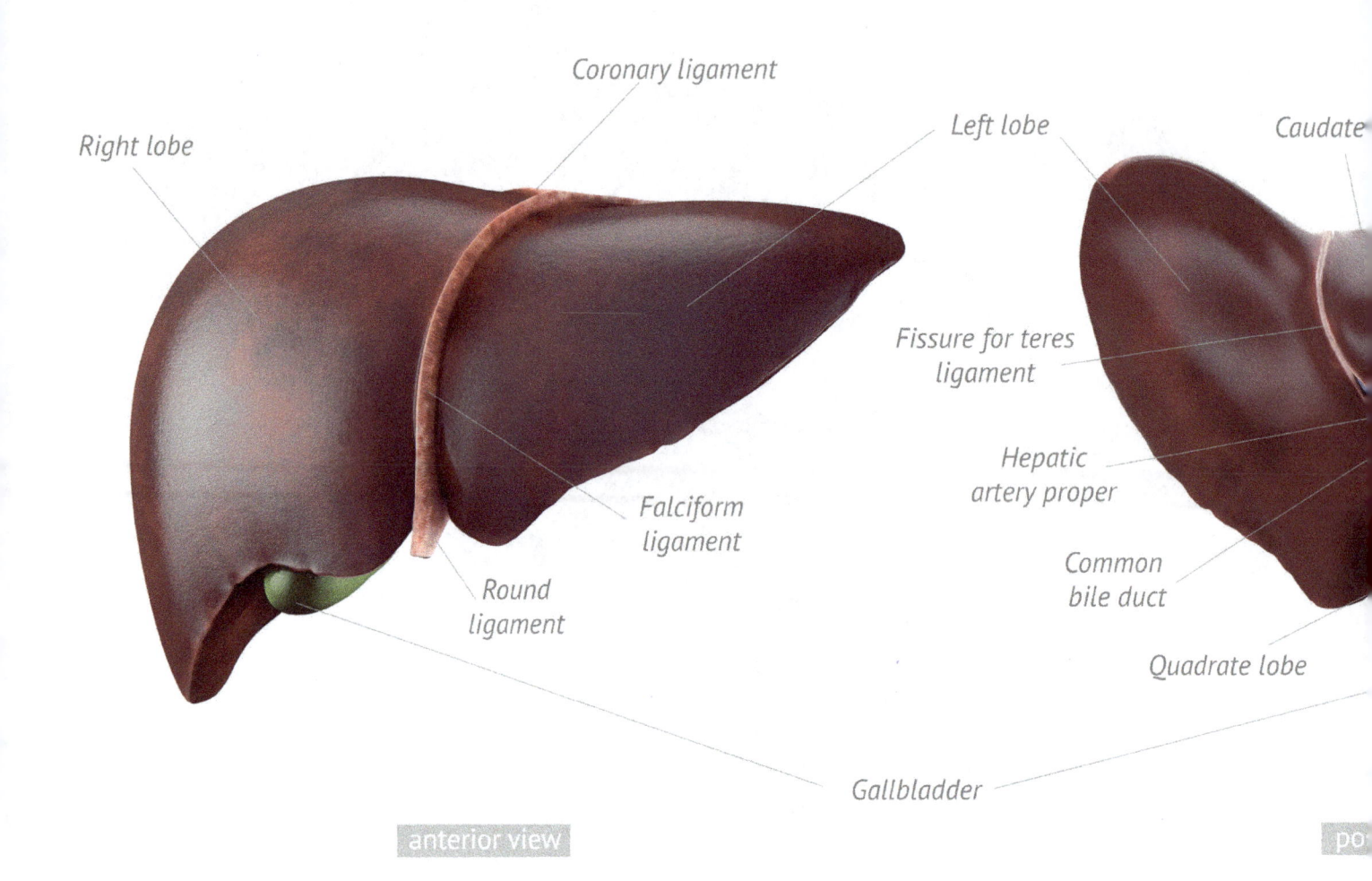

- Coronary ligament
- Right lobe
- Left lobe
- Caudate
- Fissure for teres ligament
- Falciform ligament
- Hepatic artery proper
- Round ligament
- Common bile duct
- Quadrate lobe
- Gallbladder

anterior view

ior vena cava

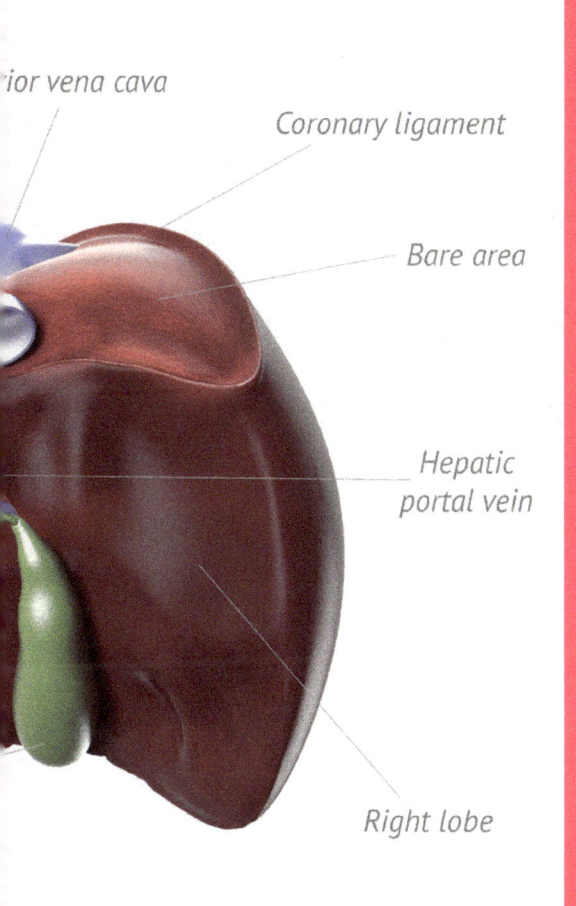

Coronary ligament

Bare area

Hepatic portal vein

Right lobe

- **LUNGS** - These are major organs that provide the much-needed oxygen to our blood stream.

- **LIVER** - The liver is responsible for all types of vital functions from assisting is breaking down food to getting rid of toxins in our bodies.

- **STOMACH** - The stomach retains food once we eat it and then secretes enzymes that help in breaking down food prior to it reaching the small intestine.

Human Stomach.

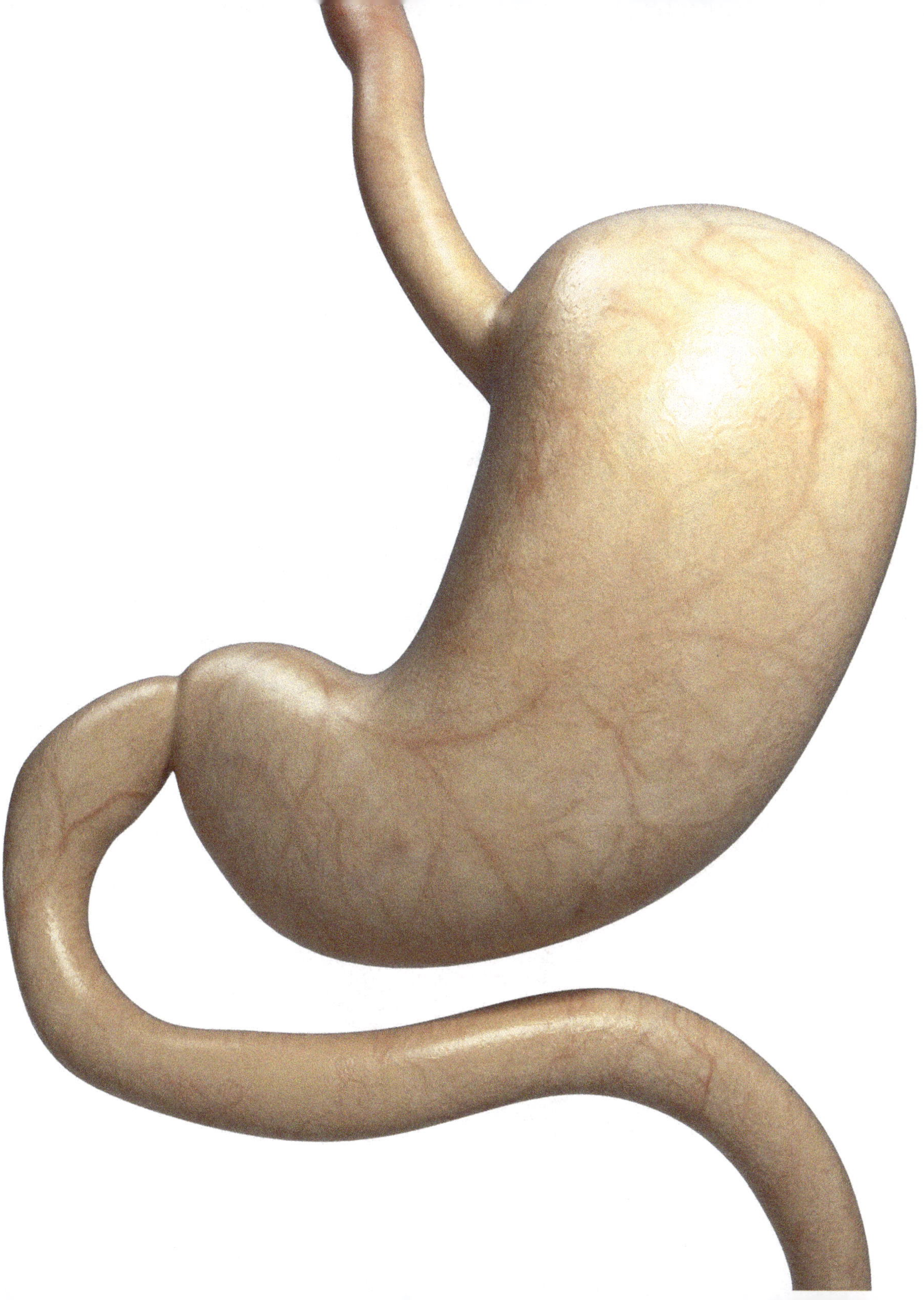

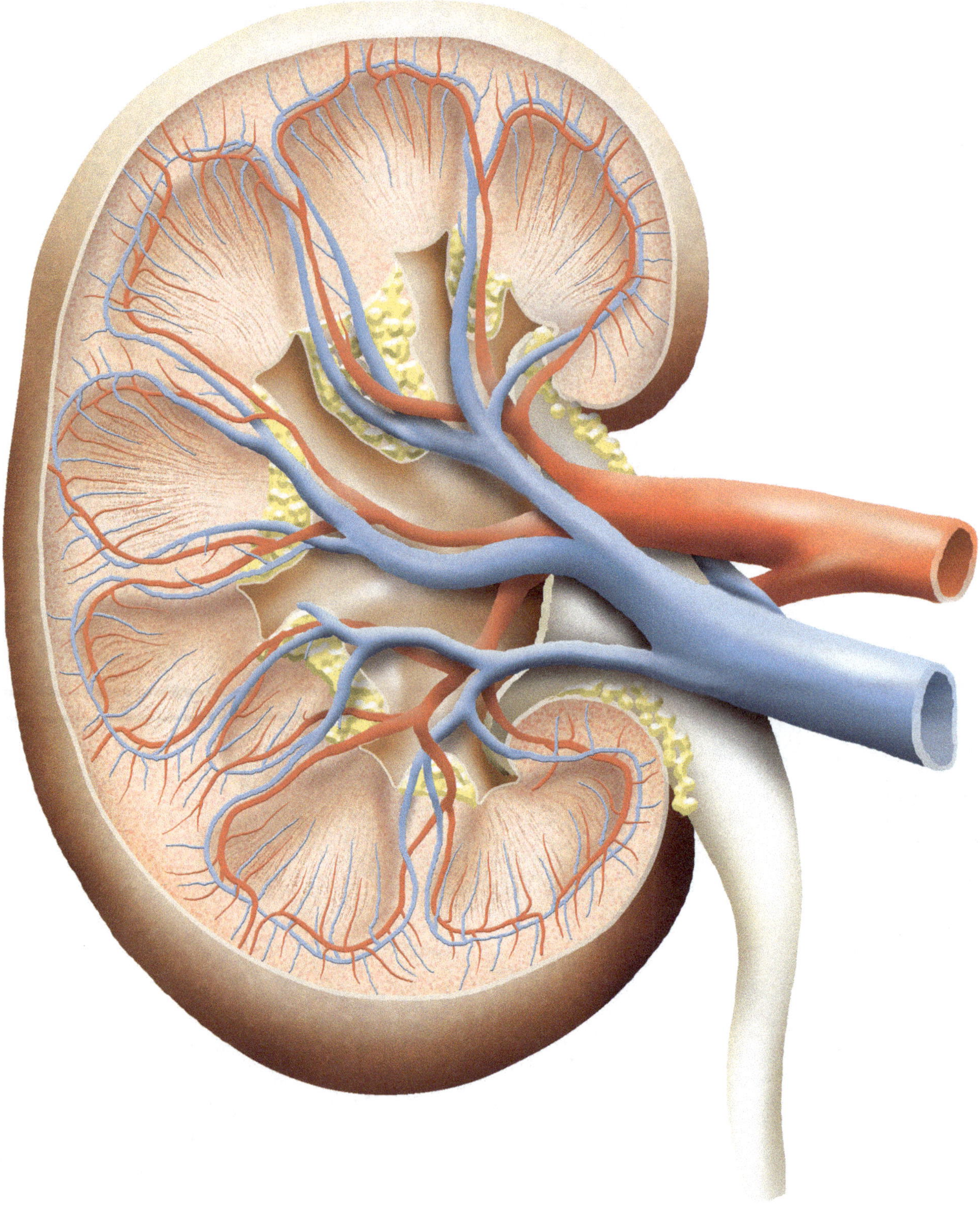

- **KIDNEYS** - The kidneys assist in keeping our bodies clean from waste products and toxins. If we did not have kidneys, our blood would become poisoned immediately.

- **HEART** - The heart is known to be the center of life. Keeping the heart healthy also assists in keeping the remaining organs and body healthy.

Human Kidney.

- **SKIN** - The skin is considered to be a major organ and covers our entire body. In addition, it provides feedback to our brain by the sense of touch.

Human skin cutaway diagram.

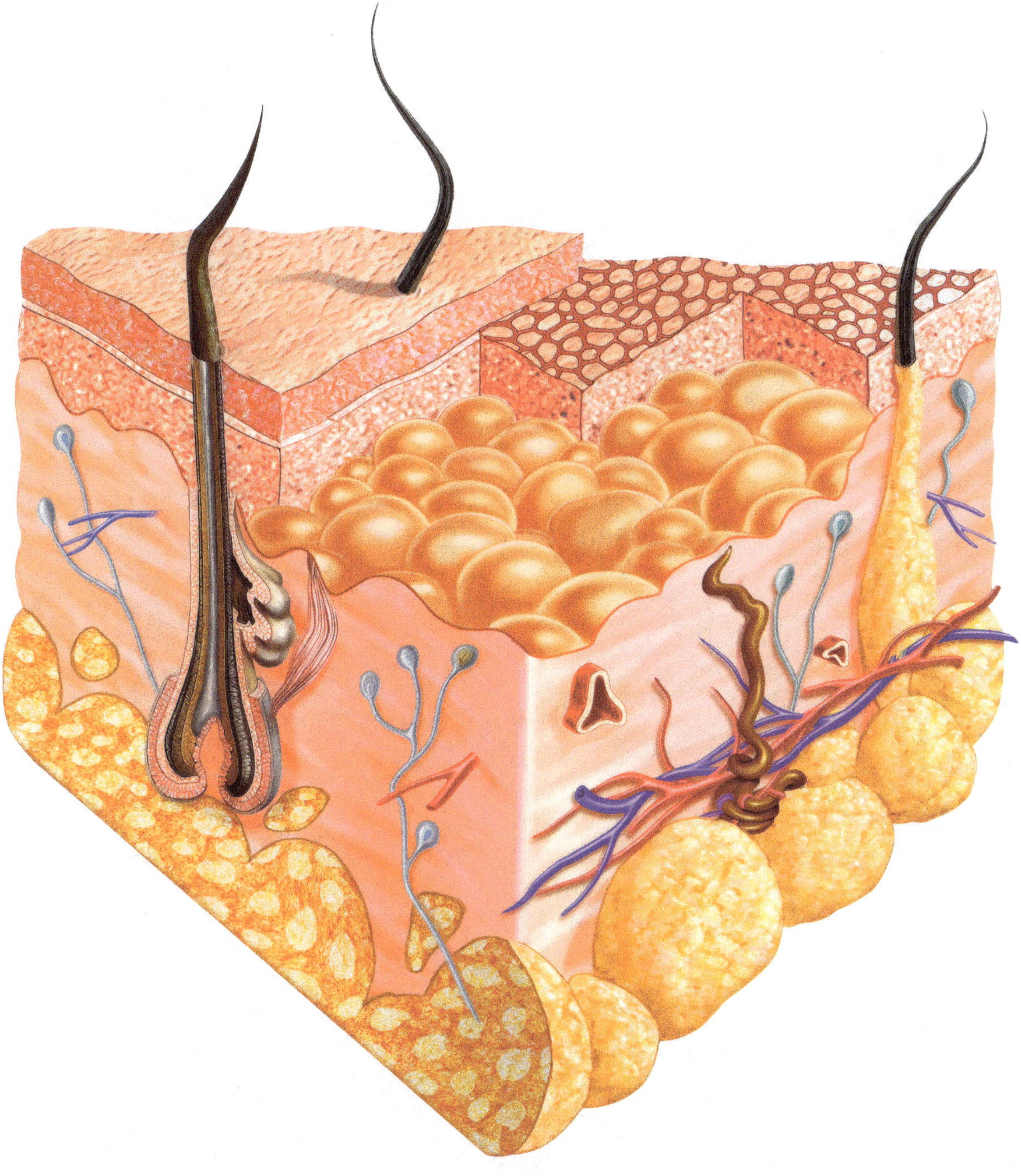

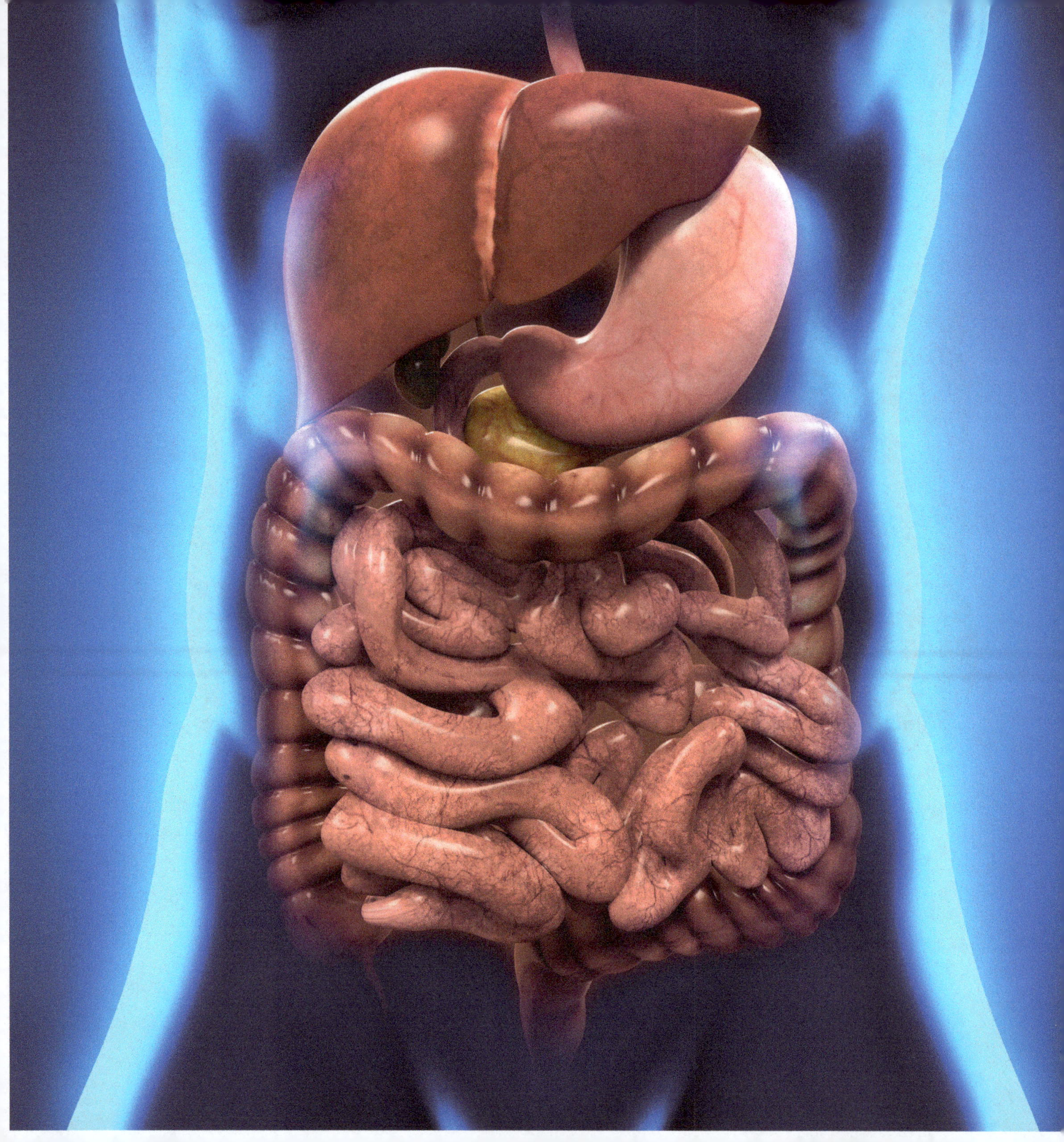

For additional information about the digestive system and the other systems in the human body you can go to your local library, research the internet, and ask questions of your teachers, family, and friends.

Human Digestive System.

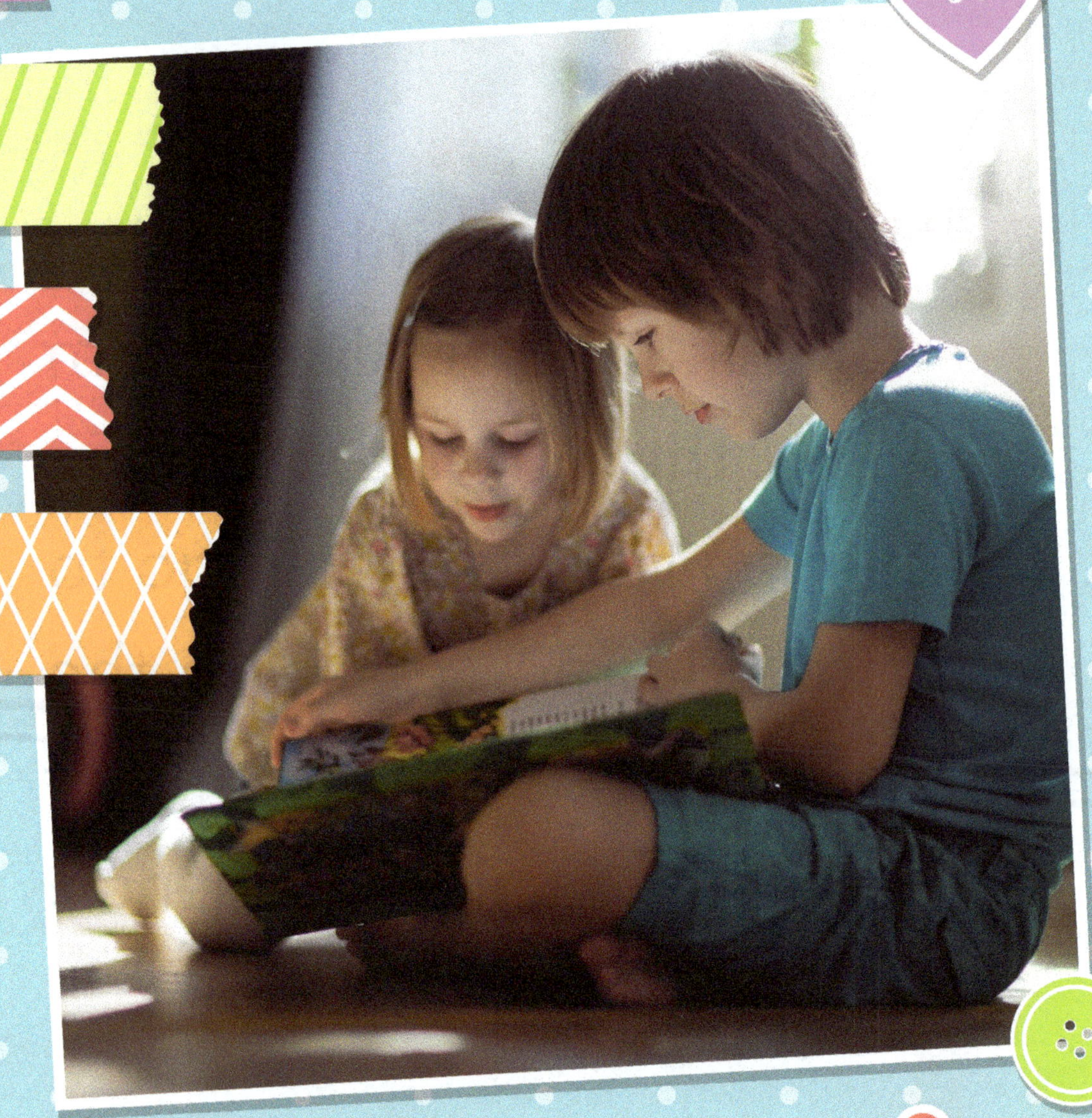

Visit

BABY PROFESSOR
EDUCATION KIDS

www.BabyProfessorBooks.com

to download Free Baby Professor eBooks and view our catalog of new and exciting Children's Books

Lightning Source UK Ltd.
Milton Keynes UK
UKHW050433130121
376927UK00006B/42